T0328801

Cambridge Elements ☰

Elements in Epistemology
edited by
Stephen Hetherington
University of New South Wales, Sydney

HIGHER-ORDER EVIDENCE AND CALIBRATIONISM

Ru Ye
Wuhan University

Shaftesbury Road, Cambridge CB2 8EA, United Kingdom

One Liberty Plaza, 20th Floor, New York, NY 10006, USA

477 Williamstown Road, Port Melbourne, VIC 3207, Australia

314–321, 3rd Floor, Plot 3, Splendor Forum, Jasola District Centre,
New Delhi – 110025, India

103 Penang Road, #05–06/07, Visioncrest Commercial, Singapore 238467

Cambridge University Press is part of Cambridge University Press & Assessment,
a department of the University of Cambridge.

We share the University's mission to contribute to society through the pursuit of
education, learning and research at the highest international levels of excellence.

www.cambridge.org
Information on this title: www.cambridge.org/9781009124195

DOI: 10.1017/9781009127332

First published 2023

A catalogue record for this publication is available from the British Library.

ISBN 978-1-009-12419-5 Paperback
ISSN 2398-0567 (online)
ISSN 2514-3832 (print)

Cambridge University Press & Assessment has no responsibility for the persistence
or accuracy of URLs for external or third-party internet websites referred to in this
publication and does not guarantee that any content on such websites is, or will
remain, accurate or appropriate.

Higher-Order Evidence and Calibrationism

Elements in Epistemology

DOI: 10.1017/9781009127332
First published online: January 2023

Ru Ye
Wuhan University
Author for correspondence: Ru Ye, ruye08@gmail.com

Abstract: The higher-order evidence debate concerns how higher-order evidence affects the rationality of our first-order beliefs. This Element has two parts. The first part (Sections 1 and 2) provides a critical overview of the literature, aiming to explain why the higher-order evidence debate is interesting and important. The second part (Sections 3 to 6) defends calibrationism, the view that we should respond to higher-order evidence by aligning our credences to our reliability degree. The author first discusses the traditional version of calibrationism and explains its main difficulties, before proposing a new version of calibrationism called 'Evidence-Discounting Calibrationism.' The Element argues that this new version is independently plausible and that it can avoid the difficulties faced by the traditional version.

Keywords: higher-order evidence, epistemic rationality, conditionalization, evidence, defeat

ISBNs: 9781009124195 (PB), 9781009127332 (OC)
ISSNs: 2398-0567 (online), 2514-3832 (print)

Contents

1 Introduction

Imagine that you're a detective working on a murder case. You have collected a large body of evidence, such as fingerprints from the crime scene and witnesses' testimonies. Based on the evidence, you believe that John is the murderer. Suppose that your belief is in fact rational. But then you are reminded that you haven't slept for days, and you know that sleep deprivation undermines people's abilities to assess evidence. Should you thereby have less confidence that John is the murderer?

This question lies at the heart of the debate on so-called higher-order evidence (HOE). Your first-order evidence regarding a belief is information that's directly about the content of your belief – it's evidence that makes the content of your belief more (or less) likely to be true. In contrast, HOE is evidence not directly about the content of your belief, but evidence about your first-order evidence or about your belief-forming process.

The central question surrounding the HOE debate is this: what exactly is the significance of HOE on our first-order beliefs? This Element aims to provide a critical review of the debate and defend a novel answer to the central question. In this introductory section, I first explain the notion of HOE and what exactly the debate on HOE is about (Sections 1.1 and 1.2). Then I explain why the debate is important and why the issue surrounding HOE is puzzling (Sections 1.3 and 1.4).

1.1 What's Higher-Order Evidence?

Roughly speaking, HOE is evidence not directly about the content of your belief, but evidence about your first-order evidence or about your belief-forming process. Before I characterize HOE more precisely, let's see two more classic examples of HOE from the literature:

Drug
I am a student in a logic class. I believe that I have just solved the logical puzzle given by the professor. But then a classmate told me that into the coffee I just had was slipped some drug that undetectably harms one's logical reasoning ability. People affected by the drug only have a 50% chance of correctly solving the logic puzzle. (Christensen, 2010, p. 187)

Hypoxia
A pilot is considering whether he has enough fuel to make it to Hawaii. Based on his past experience and his calculation of how much fuel is needed, the pilot rationally believes that he can make it to Hawaii. But then he is reminded that he is in a state of hypoxia, a condition that often undetectably harms pilots' reasoning, so that they reach the correct conclusion only 50% of the time. (Elga, n.d.)

Although scholars agree that these are typical cases of HOE, they don't characterize HOE in exactly the same way. Some characterize HOE as evidence about the *rationality* of one's belief. For example, according to Christensen (2010, p. 185) and Lasonen-Aarnio (2014, pp. 315–16), the HOE in these examples is evidence that one's belief is 'rationally sub-par' or evidence of one's 'rational failure.' Others describe HOE not as evidence about the rationality of one's belief but as evidence about one's *reliability*, namely, evidence about the objective probability of one's reaching a true belief on the basis of one's evidence (Christensen, 2016b, p. 397). Other scholars focus not on evidence about the rationality of one's belief or the reliability of the agent, but on evidence about *one's evidence*; for instance, Feldman (2005) and Worsnip (2018) use the term 'HOE' to describe evidence about the *evidential support relation* in question, or evidence about *what evidence one in fact has*.

These characterizations differ in some important respects. First, evidence about one's rationality or reliability is more 'agent-focused' than evidence about one's evidence, in the sense that they are more concerned with the agent's cognitive abilities than with the agent's evidence. For instance, one might get evidence that one's belief is formed through a process like random coin-flipping; this is evidence that one's belief is formed through an irrational and unreliable process, but it doesn't provide any evidence concerning what evidence one has or whether one's evidence supports the believed proposition – if I know that your belief that H is formed through random coin-flipping, I don't thereby get to know that your evidence doesn't support H.[1]

Second, evidence about the rationality of a belief can also come apart from evidence about the reliability of the believer.[2] If rationality is essentially the same thing as reliability, as reliabilists tend to think, then the distinction between the two kinds of evidence collapses. But if rationality is essentially a matter of conforming to what one's evidence supports, as evidentialists tend to think, then evidence about reliability will be broader than evidence about rationality. To the extent that irrational beliefs are often unlikely to be true, evidence of irrationality will often also be evidence of unreliability. But evidence of unreliability is not limited to evidence of irrationality. For example, suppose that you are a doctor, and you learn that you've been slipped some drug that makes you unreliable in noticing crucial symptoms of your patient. That is, the HOE says that you have cognitive deficiencies in *collecting* evidence, not

---

[1] See Christensen (2010)'s discussion of the 'agent-relativity' feature of HOE.

[2] See Christensen (2016a)'s distinction between the two kinds of evidence in the context of peer disagreement. He makes a distinction between disagreement with a *rationality-peer* and disagreement with an *accuracy-peer*, and argues that they provide evidence of irrationality and evidence of unreliability respectively.

cognitive deficiencies in *analyzing* the evidence you have. Such deficiencies in collecting evidence will also make you unlikely to give a correct diagnosis. So, in this case, the HOE is evidence of unreliability, but not evidence of irrationality (in the evidentialist sense of irrationality).

In sum, the term 'HOE' has been used to refer to the following different kinds of evidence: (a) evidence about the rationality of one's belief, (b) evidence about one's reliability, (c) evidence about what evidence one has, and (d) evidence about what one's evidence supports. In the detective example, your evidence is of kind (a) and (b). Clearly, that your ability in assessing evidence is impaired by sleep deprivation is not first-order evidence: it doesn't bear on whether John is the murderer. It's also not HOE of kind (c) and (d): your cognitive impairment due to sleep deprivation doesn't bear on what evidence you have or whether the evidence actually supports the proposition that John is the murderer. Rather, your cognitive impairment is evidence that, no matter what first-order evidence you have and no matter what it actually supports, it's unlikely that you can correctly assess your evidence, and thus unlikely that you can form a true belief in the circumstance.

In this Element, I will use the term 'HOE' to cover all these kinds of evidence, since one of its aims is to provide a broad review of the literature.[3] That said, some of the claims I make in the first part of this Element (Sections 1 and 2) will look more plausible for some kinds of HOE than for other kinds. I will clarify this matter in due course. And in the second part of this Element (Sections 3 to 6), where I discuss Calibrationism, I will focus on HOE about reliability, since the current discussion of Calibrationism has focused more on this kind of HOE than on other kinds.

1.2 What's the Higher-Order Evidence Debate?

The central questions in the HOE debate are these: what's the normative significance of HOE? In particular, does evidence of cognitive impairment defeat the rationality of one's first-order belief? If it defeats the rationality of one's first-order belief, how exactly does it do so?

Why are these questions important? There are at least two reasons. First, the issue of how to understand the significance of HOE is closely connected to other important debates in epistemology and in ethics. For instance, the issue lies at the heart of the debate on peer disagreement and the debate on irrelevant influences (Schoenfield, 2014; Street, 2006; Vavova, 2018; White, 2010).[4] Second, the issue is

---

[3] Existing introductions to the HOE debate include Whiting (in press) and Dorst (in press).

[4] The debate on HOE is also closely connected to the debate on moral uncertainty, which concerns what we morally should do when we are uncertain about what we morally should do. See Bykvist (2017) for a review of the debate.

itself puzzling: an intuitive position on the debate, which claims that HOE has a significant impact on one's first-order belief, creates a puzzle, and attempts at solving the puzzle have led scholars to endorse various important and surprising conclusions about epistemic rationality.

In what follows, I first explain how the debate on HOE influences other debates, and then I explain the puzzle surrounding HOE.

1.3 Connections with Other Debates

The debate on HOE originates from the debate on peer disagreement. Peers are defined to be persons with roughly the same evidence and roughly the same abilities in assessing evidence. Regarding the question of how to respond to peer disagreement, a popular view, called 'Conciliationism,' says that you should revise your doxastic attitude in the direction of your peer's (Christensen, 2009). Most importantly, it says that you should revise your doxastic attitude regardless of whether your attitude is a rational response to the original evidence. An influential argument for Conciliationism goes as follows (Christensen, 2009, p. 757). Suppose you believe that p and you learn that a peer believes that *not-p*. Then,

P_1: Learning of the peer disagreement requires you to be no more than 50 percent confident that you have correctly evaluated your evidence.
P_2: If you should be no more than 50 percent confident that you have correctly evaluated your evidence, you should withdraw your belief that p.
So,
C. Learning the peer disagreement requires withdrawing your belief that p.

Premise P_1 is motivated as follows. Given that you are peers, when you disagree, you should think that the probability that you have correctly evaluated your evidence equals the probability that your peer has; assuming that these two possibilities are mutually exclusive (i.e., you and your peer cannot both have correctly evaluated your evidence),[5] you cannot be more than 50 percent confident that you have correctly evaluated your evidence. Premise P_2 is motivated by a so-called level-bridging principle. A common formulation of this principle says that one's attitude on the higher-order proposition about whether one's belief is rational should match one's attitude on the relevant first-order proposition. So, if you should be no more than 50 percent confident that you have correctly evaluated your evidence, you should no longer believe that p.

---

[5] This assumption is controversial. See the debate on the so-called Uniqueness Thesis (Kelly, 2014; White, 2005).

This argument for Conciliationism essentially says that peer disagreement provides a kind of HOE, and that HOE has a significant impact on one's first-order belief. The main alternative to Conciliationism, known as the Steadfast View, denies the impact of HOE on one's first-order belief. It says that what doxastic attitude is rational is primarily determined by what one's first-order evidence supports. So, how the significance of HOE is understood greatly affects the debate between Conciliationism and the Steadfast View.

The HOE debate is also tightly connected to the debate on irrelevant influence (Vavova, 2018; White, 2010) This debate concerns this question: When one learns that one's beliefs are influenced by factors that are irrelevant to the truth (factors such as evolutionary forces or one's upbringing), should one retract one's beliefs? How this question is answered clearly depends on how the significance of HOE is understood, since evidence about the origin of one's belief is a kind of HOE – it's not evidence bearing on the content of one's belief, but on whether one's belief is formed in a reliable or rational way.

1.4 A Puzzle about Higher-Order Evidence

The issue of how to understand the significance of HOE is puzzling. To illustrate, let's consider the following dramatic case of HOE. Suppose that you initially believe that p and suppose that this belief is rational because it's supported by your first-order evidence E. Then you receive a piece of HOE saying that you have been slipped a drug that causes people to make judgments about p through a process like random coin-flipping, although it seems to those people that their judgments are based on rational assessment of evidence.

In this case, the HOE seems to require you to give up your initial belief. However, it's unclear why the HOE is able to do so. After all, evidence that you form judgments about p in a random coin-flipping way is not evidence against p; nor is it evidence undermining the support relation that E bears on p – that you are a coin-flipper just says nothing about the evidential connection between E and p. The evidential connection is some *logical, statistical, or explanatory relation* between E and p. Such relations are not affected by matters of how you form beliefs about p. For instance, suppose that you originally believe p because you think that E is best explained by the truth of p; then when you get the HOE saying that you are drugged, you don't get to say, 'E is *not* best explained by the truth of p.' Whether E is best explained by p seems to have nothing to do with whether you are drugged.

To further explain this point that the HOE doesn't undermine the evidential connection between E and p, let's fill in this drug case with more details. Imagine that you are a detective deliberating on whether Jack is the murderer.

Your evidence includes fingerprints collected from the crime scene and witnesses' testimonies. After carefully analyzing the evidence, you come to believe that the evidence is best explained by Jack's being the murderer. Then you receive HOE saying that you are drugged so that you form beliefs about homicide cases in a random coin-flipping way, even though things seem perfectly normal to you. Clearly, you should not now think, 'I guess the fingerprints and the witnesses' testimonies are not best explained by Jack's being the murderer after all.' In contrast, in a classic undercutting-evidence case, the evidential connection is undermined and a change in your view of the evidential connection is reasonable. For instance, if instead of being told that you have been drugged, you are told that the fingerprints are planted and the witnesses are unreliable (say, they have poor eyesight), then this *will* undermine the explanatory relation in question, and you should now think that the original evidence is not best explained by Jack's being the murderer.

In this case, the evidence that you are being drugged so that you are effectively a random coin-flipper is a typical case of HOE about an agent's unreliability. This kind of HOE says that you are unlikely to reach a true belief about the proposition in question due to a drug, sleep deprivation, hallucination, or some other condition that impairs cognitive abilities, without being evidence about whether the proposition is true or whether it's supported by your original evidence. To put it another way, this kind of HOE is evidence about *your* cognitive ability. That *you* are unlikely to reach a true belief about the proposition or about the evidential connection in question tells us little about whether the proposition is true or whether the evidential connection is there.

Let's return to the explanation of why HOE creates a puzzle. I have explained that, in the drug case, your HOE *doesn't* undermine the original evidential connection – that is, your original evidence E *still* supports p. But if E still supports p, and if the HOE doesn't provide any evidence against p, then it seems that your new total evidence E&HOE also supports p. Then how come you are required to give up the belief that p? So, to say that the HOE requires you to give up your initial belief seems to conflict with a broadly evidentialist requirement on rational beliefs.

But a plausible case *can* be made for our intuition that you should give up your initial belief when gaining the HOE. It seems that the HOE requires you to adopt a higher-order belief 'it's unlikely that I form a correct belief about p.' But if you hold this belief, it seems that you should not continue to believe that p. The idea is that it seems self-incoherent to continue to believe that p while believing that the cognitive process underlying that belief is essentially a random coin-flipping.

This discussion reveals a conflict between the following two plausible principles of epistemic rationality:[6]

Evidentialism

One's belief that p is rational if and only if it's supported by one's total evidence.

Bridging

It's irrational for one to believe that p and also believe that the cognitive process underlying the belief is unreliable.

The two principles seem to be in conflict because it seems that your total evidence E&HOE can both support p and support a higher-order proposition saying that the cognitive process underlying the belief p is unreliable. As we have seen in the drug case, your total evidence E&HOE still supports p, since the HOE doesn't undermine the support relation between E and p and since it doesn't provide any evidence against p. But E&HOE also supports the relevant higher-order proposition: the HOE supports this higher-order proposition, and the first-order evidence E only bears on whether p and says nothing about your reliability or any other person's reliability. So, in the drug case, obeying Evidentialism with regard to both the first-order belief p and the higher-order belief requires violating Bridging.

Now, as I've explained in Section 1.1, there are various types of HOE discussed in the literature: evidence about one's reliability, evidence about the rationality of one's belief, evidence about what evidence one has, and evidence about the relevant evidential connection. The discussion has explained how HOE about one's reliability can generate a puzzle. While I think that the puzzle is most salient for this type of HOE, some scholars have argued that a similar puzzle – namely, a conflict between Evidentialism and a similar level-bridging principle – can also be generated by other kinds of HOE. For instance, Worsnip (2018) has argued that the puzzle arises for HOE about the evidential connection between E and p. According to Worsnip, the puzzle arises because one's total evidence can be misleading about what it supports; that is, one's evidence can both support p and support that it doesn't support p, so that obeying Evidentialism can lead to violation of the following plausible principle:

Enkrasia

It's irrational for one to believe p and also believe that one's evidence doesn't support p.

---

[6] Another interesting puzzle surrounding HOE is 'the Fumerton's Puzzle' for theories of rationality, which says that if HOE affects one's first-order belief, then there can be no sufficient condition for rationality. See Foley (1990), Lasonen-Aarnio (2014), Sepielli (2014), and Ye (2015) for discussion of the puzzle.

You might wonder whether your total evidence can really be misleading about what it supports; that is, can it really support p but also support 'my total evidence doesn't support p?' The answer here is not as clear as it is in the case of HOE about one's unreliability. While it's intuitive that evidence of one's unreliability (e.g., evidence that one is a coin-flipper) doesn't undermine the evidential support E bears on p, evidence that E doesn't support p does seem to undermine the support.

However, at least on some prominent understanding of evidence and the evidential support relation (e.g., Williamson's knowledge conception of evidence and the 'high evidential probability' conception of evidential support), your total evidence can indeed be misleading about what it supports. A famous case illustrating this possibility is Horowitz's (2014) 'Dartboard' case, which originates from Williamson's 'Unmarked Clock' case (Williamson, 2000, p. 229):

> Dartboard
> You have a large, blank dartboard. When you throw a dart at the board, it can only land at grid points, which are spaced one inch apart along the horizontal and vertical axes. (It can only land at grid points because the dartboard is magnetic, and it's only magnetized at those points.) Although you are pretty good at picking out where the dart has landed, you are rationally highly confident that your discrimination is not perfect: in particular, you are confident that when you judge where the dart has landed, you might mistake its position for one of the points an inch away (i.e. directly above, below, to the left, or to the right). You are also confident that, wherever the dart lands, you will know that it has *not* landed at any point farther away than one of those four. You throw a dart, and it lands on a point somewhere close to the middle of the board. (Horowitz, 2014, p. 736)

Suppose the dart landed at point <3,3>, and consider the proposition *Ring*: the dart landed on one of <3,2>, <2,3>, <4,3>, or <3,4>. Then your evidence supports a high 0.8 credence in *Ring*, since it's true in four out of five epistemic possibilities, and we assume that each epistemic possibility is equally likely. But your evidence also supports a high 0.8 credence in 'my evidence supports a 0.2 credence in *Ring*,' since this higher-order proposition is also true in four out of five of your epistemic possibilities. So, if we claim that your evidence supports p just in case its evidential probability is not lower than 0.8 (which is an arbitrary choice, since we can construct a similar case for other thresholds), this is a case where your total evidence is misleading about whether it supports a proposition p. (For further discussion of cases like Dartboard, see Elga [2013], Skipper [2019], and Worsnip [2018].)

So, it seems that, just like Evidentialism can come into conflict with Bridging, it can also come into conflict with Enkrasia, and this conflict is puzzling since these principles are all intuitively plausible. However, I should note that some authors have expressed doubts about the alleged puzzle. For instance, Skipper (2021) has argued that, although one's HOE can be misleading about one's *first-order evidence* supports, it can never be misleading about what one's *total evidence* supports. Dorst (2020) has argued that if we replace Enkrasia with a more plausible level-connecting principle that he calls 'Trust,' then we no longer have a conflict with Evidentialism. More attempts at solving the puzzle will be discussed in Section 2.

To sum up this section, HOE generates a puzzle: both Evidentialism and Bridging (or Enkrasia) are plausible and yet they seem to come into conflict. What's worse, *the puzzle doesn't merely arise for evidentialists*: it generalizes to a wide range of theories about determinants of rationality. Suppose we say that rationality is determined by some condition C. For a wide range of candidate condition C, it's possible that both your first-order belief p and the relevant higher-order belief satisfy C, just like it's possible that they can both be supported by evidence. For instance, it's possible that both your belief p and your belief 'my belief p is produced by an unreliable process' are produced by a reliable process. So, it's not just the evidentialist who faces the puzzle. However, for simplicity, I will continue to use the evidentialist presentation of the puzzle in my following discussion.

2 Major Positions in the Higher-Order Evidence Debate

In Section 1, we have seen that there is an apparent conflict between Evidentialism and Bridging. We have seen that the conflict arises because:

(a) Given your total evidence, you should believe that your belief that p is unreliably formed (or irrational, or not supported by your evidence, etc.).
(b) Given your total evidence, you should believe that p.
(c) Given plausible level-connecting principles (such as Bridging or Enkrasia), you should not hold both beliefs.

There is an apparent conflict among the three claims. Major positions in the HOE debate can be structured around how they respond to the conflict. I critically review the three main positions in this section.

2.1 Higher-Order Defeat/Calibrationism

The first response to the puzzle is called 'Higher-Order Defeat.' It says that HOE defeats the rationality of one's first-order belief. That is, it keeps (a) and (c) but denies (b) (Christensen, 2010; Feldman, 2005; Neta, 2018; Skipper, 2019). There are several explanations of how the Higher-Order Defeat happens.

The first is an idea of 'bracketing': even though E is evidence about p, the HOE of your unreliability or irrationality requires you to *set aside* E in reasoning about p. (Christensen [2010] first proposes this idea of bracketing in discussing how to respond to HOE about one's unreliability.) Since we assume that E is all the first-order evidence you have, bracketing E means that you can no longer rationally believe that p.

The motivation for the bracketing view can be seen with the following analogy. Consider a knife you use as a tool for cutting things. One situation where you should not use the knife is when you know that it's broken so that it can no longer function as a good tool for cutting. But another situation where you should not use the knife is when you gain evidence saying that you've developed some brain disease so that your hands will shake uncontrollably when you use the knife. Moreover, it seems that you should not use the knife in this situation even if the evidence about your brain disease is in fact misleading. Similarly, we can consider evidence as the tool we use for the purpose of forming true beliefs. One situation where you should not use a piece of evidence in forming beliefs about p is when you know that its usual evidential link to p is broken (which is what happens when you gain undermining evidence). However, another situation where you should not use the evidence is when you gain evidence saying that you suffer from some cognitive impairment so that your chance of forming true beliefs on the basis of that evidence is very low. Moreover, it seems that you should not use the evidence in this situation even if the evidence about your cognitive impairment is in fact misleading.

The idea behind the analogy is simple: in the knife case, when gaining evidence about the brain disease, you shouldn't trust yourself to properly use the knife for the purpose of cutting; similarly, in the cognitive case, when gaining HOE about your unreliability, you shouldn't trust yourself to properly use the evidence about p for the purpose of forming true beliefs about p.[7]

The second explanation of how Higher-Order Defeat happens involves 'evidence dispossession': when you have HOE, you no longer *possess* E as available evidence about p. (See Gonzalez de Prado [2020] for an explicit defense of this view; Greco [2019] can also be read as a defense of this view.) The motivation for this view is that for a proposition E to be evidence you possess, you must satisfy a certain epistemic condition with regard to E – a proposition doesn't count as evidence you possess if you are utterly unaware of it. Traditionally, the epistemic conditions say that you must *be aware of* E, or

---

[7] For a detailed explanation of why we should do the bracketing, see Ye (2020), who argues that it's intellectually irresponsible to rely on the evidence that one thinks one is unable to make proper use of.

rationally believe E, or *know* E. However, Gonzalez de Prado (2020) defends the following epistemic condition:

> Competence
> If a person is not in a position to competently treat that *p* as evidence that *q*, she doesn't possess that *p* as evidence that *q*.

Then Gonzalez de Prado (2020) argues that when one gains HOE of unreliability, the competence condition is no longer satisfied with respect to E, so that one no longer possesses E as evidence for *p*.

Both kinds of explanations are not fully satisfactory as they stand. About the evidence dispossession explanation, I find it hard to believe that evidence of your unreliability makes you dispossess the original evidence. Consider the analogy with the knife. It's hard to believe that you dispossess the knife when you gain evidence that you cannot properly use the knife due to your brain disease. And Gonzalez de Prado's competence account doesn't strike me as helpful. Even if competence is a constraint on evidence-possession, it's unclear why gaining HOE makes one lose the competence. If one is originally competent in treating E as reasons for *p*, in the sense that one is sensitive to E in one's belief-revision with regard to *p*, it seems that one can still be competent when gaining the HOE. Again, the analogy with the knife is illustrative: if you are originally competent in using the knife for cutting, then it's unclear how gaining (misleading) evidence that you are incompetent due to your brain disease will make you lose the competence.

About the bracketing explanation, critics of Higher-Order Defeat have raised the following worries. First, it makes the phenomenon of Higher-Order Defeat inconsistent with Bayesianism about rational credence, because it implies that we should sometimes violate probabilism and conditionalization (White, 2009). I will explain this challenge further in Sections 4 and 5.

Second, according to Kelly (2010) and Schoenfield (2015), to say that one should bracket first-order evidence is to say that what the first-order evidence supports is entirely irrelevant to rationality when one gains HOE; that is, what's rational to believe is determined by one's HOE alone, and this is problematic because 'it makes rationality come by too easily' (Kelly, 2010). I will explain this worry in greater detail in Section 4; here, I only explain the basic idea.

Why will bracketing first-order evidence make rationality come by too easily? Basically, it's because it's very easy to gain HOE, and for many proponents of the Higher-Order Defeat view, there is a simple recipe telling us how to respond to the gained HOE. For example, you can easily gain HOE on a controversial topic by exchanging views with an epistemic peer. And according to many proponents of Conciliationism (which can be regarded the Higher-Order Defeat view applied to cases of peer disagreement – see Section 1.3), there is a simple recipe of how to respond to the gained HOE: you simply split the difference with your peer. Such a recipe is much easier to follow than the opaque, Steadfastness View's recommendation 'Proportion your credence with the one supported by your first-order evidence!' So, even if you start out with an irrational credence relative to your first-order evidence, you can easily adopt the rational credence relative to your total evidence by splitting the difference with a peer who holds a different credence. To make the case more dramatic, we can imagine that both you and your peer start out with irrational credence. Imagine that you start out with credence 0.2 in p and your peer starts out with credence 0.6, while the rational credence supported by the shared first-order evidence is 0.9. Then Conciliationism says that both of you will adopt a rational credence simply by adopting credence 0.4. So, a weird thing happens: two irrational persons become rational simply because they have met with each other!

Kelly raises the ignoring-evidence worry in the context of peer disagreement, but the worry generalizes to other cases of HOE. However, to explain the general worry adequately, it's helpful to consider a view of HOE that extends the Higher-Order Defeat view from the negative, defeating kind of HOE to the positive kind of HOE (i.e., HOE that says that you are highly reliable or rational). One such view is called 'Calibrationism.' I will explain this view in greater detail later, but basically, it says that the rational credence is the one that matches the so-called degree of expected reliability. Since information of expected reliability is easy to come by (basically, you can gain the information just by examining your past track record to see how frequently you believe the truth), Calibrationism will also imply that what the first-order evidence supports is irrelevant and that rationality is easy to come by.

Here is a third worry about the bracketing proposal: it seems to conflict with the principle of not ignoring free evidence. To see the conflict, let's imagine a case where you have HOE but no first-order evidence yet. Suppose that you can choose whether to get some free first-order evidence about p, although you don't know exactly what that evidence is, and suppose that your HOE says that you are unreliable in correctly evaluating the evidence, whatever that evidence is. Then, according to the argument that motivates the bracketing proposal, you should choose not to gather the free evidence, since you cannot trust yourself to properly use it for the purpose of gaining truths. But this conflicts with the famous 'Good's Theorem,' which says that, if one can choose between acting on the basis of one's current evidence and acting after one gains additional, free evidence, one should choose the latter, because it has greater expected utility (Good, 1967).

Despite the above three worries, I think that the bracketing proposal is the best existing explanation of why HOE defeats the rationality of one's first-order belief. In Section 6, I will argue that the above challenges to the bracketing proposal can be met. Moreover, I will defend a variation of Calibrationism. Calibrationism roughly says that one's credence in a proposition p should cohere with one's expected reliability concerning whether p. And according to the most common formulation of the view, this means:

> If, independently of the first-order reasoning in question, your expected reliability concerning whether p is r, then your credence in p should be r. (Schoenfield, 2015, p. 428)

Your expected reliability concerning whether p is the probability that it's rational for you to assign to the proposition that you form a correct judgment concerning whether p on the basis of your first-order evidence. (It could be calculated as your expectation of the objective probability that you form a correct judgment concerning whether p on the basis of your first-order evidence.)[8] Influential discussion of Calibrationism includes Christensen (2016b), Elga (2007), Horowitz and Sliwa (2015), Isaacs (2021), Roush (2009), Schoenfield (2015, 2018), and White (2009).

Calibrationism generalizes the view of Higher-Order Defeat. Higher-Order Defeat essentially says that one's HOE of unreliability defeats the rationality of one's original belief that p. Calibrationism implies this claim: if one has HOE of unreliability, then independent of one's first-order reasoning, one's expected reliability concerning whether p is low, and thus, by Calibrationism, one's credence in p should also be low, which means that one can no longer rationally believe that p. Calibrationism also has a broader scope than Higher-Order Defeat, since it also tells us what to do when the expected reliability is *high* (i.e., when the HOE is not a negative, potentially defeating kind of evidence.)

A motivation for Calibrationism goes as follows (see Schoenfield, 2015, p. 426; I will give more motivations in Section 3). Consider the case of Hypoxia mentioned in Section 1.1:

> Hypoxia
> A pilot is considering whether he has enough fuel to make it to Hawaii. Based on his past experience and his calculation of how much fuel is needed, the pilot rationally believes that he can make it to Hawaii. But then he is reminded that he is in a state of hypoxia, a condition that often undetectably harms pilots' reasoning, so that they reach the correct conclusion only 50% of the time. (Elga, n.d.)

---

[8] A note of clarification: I formulate Calibrationism as the view that to calibrate one's credence to expected reliability is *fully* rational. So, strictly speaking, Christensen (2010, 2016a) doesn't belong to this camp – he thinks that, although calibration is more rational than being steadfast, it still falls short of full rationality. See my introduction of the Dilemma View in Section 2.2.

It's intuitive that, in Hypoxia, the pilot should revise his credence in the proposition 'I have enough fuel to get to Hawaii' to 0.5. But there seems to be nothing special about the number 0.5 here; that is, if we change the example so that the pilot's reliability is 60 percent, then it will be tempting to say that the pilot's credence in the proposition should be 0.6. So, it's tempting to say that, in general, one's credence in the proposition one judges to be true should match the expected reliability of one's judgment.

2.2 Dilemma/Ambiguous Rationality/Second-Best Epistemology

The second response to the puzzle of HOE is to admit that there is a genuine conflict between Evidentialism and Bridging and that we should keep all of (a), (b), and (c). That is, cases of HOE give rise to epistemic dilemmas. According to Christensen (2007, 2016a), we should accept both principles as rational requirements, and sometimes different rational requirements cannot both be realized, just like sometimes different moral requirements cannot both be realized.

A variant of the dilemma view is the 'ambiguous-rationality' view. Like the dilemma view, it admits that the puzzle shows a conflict between two rationality requirements. Unlike the dilemma view, it maintains that the conflict is between different kinds of rationality; that is, Evidentialism is about one kind of rationality and Bridging is about another kind of rationality. So, the conflict is similar to the familiar conflict between different domains of evaluation. For instance, we see a conflict between epistemic rationality and prudential rationality, when one has excellent evidence supporting a belief but holding the belief has bad practical consequences.

There are different ways of cashing out the ambiguous-rationality view. According to Worsnip (2018), the ambiguity is between 'rationality in the sense of responding to evidence' and 'rationality in the sense of coherence.' According to Schoenfield (2015), the ambiguity is between 'rationality in the sense of responding to reasons' and 'rationality in the sense of reasoning well.' According to Dipaolo (2019), the ambiguity is between 'rationality in the sense of responding to evidence in the best way' and 'rationality in a second-best sense, when one cannot perform rationally in the best way.'

In my view, the dilemma view faces an explanatory challenge: assuming that requirements of epistemic rationality (no matter whether they are about a unifying sense or disunifying senses of rationality) are all grounded in a *single* epistemic value, namely, truth,[9] how could it be possible that these

---

[9] I take this truth-monism to be a popular view about epistemic values. This view is not uncontroversial, however; some claim that knowledge is the single goal of beliefs, and some are pluralists. See Pritchard (2014) and the references therein.

requirements come into conflict? Admitting moral dilemmas doesn't give rise to this challenge – since there are *multiple* moral values, neither of which seems more fundamental than others, it's easy to imagine a case where realizing one value requires one act and realizing another value requires a different act. Similarly, it's easy to see why requirements of epistemic rationality can conflict with requirements of prudential rationality, because the two domains involve distinct kind of values (say, truth and happiness). But such kind of explanation appealing to conflict between values is not available when we say that requirements of epistemic rationality come into conflict. Here is why.

First, it's hard to believe all these requirements of epistemic rationality are *fundamental*; rather, it seems that all are grounded in our value of truth – it seems that we want to follow evidence and we want to be coherent *both* because we want truth. Second, it's hard to see how a single source of value can generate conflicting requirements. If we should obey Evidentialism because following evidence is a good way of getting the truth, and if we should also obey Bridging because it's also a good way of getting the truth, then it's hard to see how there could be a dilemma: either obeying Evidentialism is more truth-conducive than obeying Bridging, or it's the other way around, or they are equally truth-conducive, or they are noncomparable in the sense that the two norms are truth-conducive in different senses of truth-conduciveness. But no matter which is the case, we don't have a dilemma. In the first two cases, only one norm is rationally required; in the third case, obeying either norm is rationally permissible; in the fourth case, we have a case of ambiguity, not a dilemma.

Besides this explanatory challenge, the dilemma view faces an additional problem: it underestimates the ubiquity of HOE. Note that HOE can be any information about your rationality or reliability, and it doesn't have to be a negative kind of evidence. Such kind of evidence is easily available if we just look at our track record and examine how frequently we've believed the truths or how frequently we've rationally assessed our evidence. This creates a problem for the dilemma view: a natural way of generalizing Bridging is to require a match between one's credence and one's expected reliability. But in general, the credence that matches expected reliability is not the one supported by one's total evidence regarding the proposition in question, or at least, we have no reason to expect that one's expected reliability degree is always identical to the degree of evidential support. (Recall my explanation in Section 1.4 about why evidence of unreliability doesn't need to undermine the evidential link between the first-order evidence and the proposition in question, so that your total evidence can still support the proposition when gaining HOE of unreliability.) Therefore, an apparent conflict between Bridging and Evidentialism is constant in our epistemic life. This makes the dilemma view hard to accept: it might be fine if epistemic dilemmas are rare; it's much harder to accept that we are constantly in epistemic dilemmas.[10]

2.3 Right Reasons/Steadfastness/Level-Splitting/Indefeasibilism

The third response to the conflict between Evidentialism and Bridging is to claim that we should maintain our first-order belief when gaining HOE. This position is known as the 'Right Reasons View' or 'Steadfastness.' It's divided into two camps, depending on how the rationality of our higher-order beliefs is viewed. The first camp is called 'Level-Splitting': both our first-order belief and our higher-order belief (of our irrationality or unreliability) are rational and thus Bridging has to go (Hazlett, 2012; Lasonen-Aarnio, 2020; Weatherson, n.d.; Williamson, 2011). The second camp is called 'Indefeasibilism': if our first-order belief is indeed rational, it's rational to think that it's rational, and no amount of HOE can defeat that rationality and require us to hold a contrary higher-order belief (Littlejohn, 2018; Titelbaum, 2015).

Level-Splitting is typically motivated by sympathies towards the externalist theories of rationality. In Section 1, we've seen why some scholars think that one's total evidence can be misleading about what it supports. In particular, the Dartboard case (Section 1.4) explains how one's evidence can support a high confidence in p and also a high confidence in 'my evidence doesn't support a high confidence in p.' In that case, the possibility of self-misleadingness in evidence arises because one can be uncertain what one's total evidence is. And uncertainty about one's evidence is typically motivated by externalist theories of evidence, such as Williamson's theory that one's evidence is one's knowledge. Besides externalist theories of evidence, it's been argued that externalist theories of rationality in general tend to give rise to level-splitting (Lasonen-Aarnio, 2010). For instance, it's easy to imagine a scenario where both one's first-order belief p and the higher-order belief 'it's irrational to believe p' are both formed through a reliable process.

Level-Splitting views have been criticized on two grounds. First, the externalism-based motivations for level-splitting and for denying Higher-Order Defeat seem to be overkill – externalism not only tends to rule out Higher-Order Defeat, but also tends to rule out other familiar, relatively uncontroversial kinds of defeat, such as rebutting and undermining (Beddor, 2015). Second, Level-Splitting leads to epistemic akrasia (i.e., that phenomenon that one

---

[10] There are two additional worries about the dilemma view, both of which are discussed in detail in Skipper (2022). First, the dilemma view is inconsistent with the conjunction of the deontic principle of agglomeration and a plausible 'ought-implies-can' principle. Second, the view is extensionally inadequate, since it doesn't give the intuitively plausible verdict that one should give up one's original belief in typical cases of HOE.

believes that p and also believes that one shouldn't believe that p), and it's hard to explain away our strong intuition against akrasia (Horowitz, 2014).

The other camp of the Right Reasons View, Indefeasibilism, is typically motivated on the ground that evidential support relations are a priori (Ichikawa & Jarvis, 2013, chap. 7; Smithies, 2015), and a priori reasons are indefeasible. If one's first-order evidence indeed supports p, one has a priori reason for believing that it supports p, and no amount of HOE that says otherwise can defeat the reason.

One problem with Indefeasibilism is this: even if evidential support relations are a priori and even if a priori reasons are indefeasible, it doesn't mean that one has indefeasible reason to believe 'my total evidence supports p' when one's total evidence indeed supports p. For to judge what one's evidence supports, one needs to judge both what one's evidence is and whether that evidence supports p. So, even if one has indefeasible reason to believe 'E supports p' when E in fact supports p, it doesn't follow that one has indefeasible reason to believe 'my total evidence supports p' – one might not have indefeasible reason to believe that E is indeed one's total evidence. Of course, it's a controversial issue whether one always has indefeasible reason to believe the truths about what one's total evidence is. In particular, an internalist of epistemic rationality might think that such truths are always luminous, such that one can always be certain of what one's total evidence is.[11] So, I acknowledge that this worry has only limited force.

A second problem with Indefeasibilism is that it's hard to generalize the view to HOE about one's unreliability. As I have explained in making the distinction between evidence of unreliability and evidence of irrationality in Section 1.1, even if one is a perfect evidence-analyst, one might still be unreliable due to deficiencies in collecting evidence. So not all factors that contribute to unreliability are about deficiencies in analyzing evidential relations. (To see this, just consider a blind person. A blind person might have perfect reasoning abilities, that is, *given* the set of perceptual information he does collect, he is capable of analyzing what that information supports; however, he might still not be as reliable in forming true perceptual beliefs as a normal person, since he might not do well in collecting perceptual information.) But unlike facts about evidential support relation, facts about one's reliability are obviously a posteriori and beliefs about these facts are clearly defeasible. Even if one is in fact reliable, one might still get strong HOE that requires one to believe that one is not.

To conclude Sections 1 and 2, the debate on HOE is about whether and how HOE affects the rationality of one's first-order belief. This debate is important because of its close connection with other important debates, such as disagreement

---

[11] For a detailed discussion of the internalist argument for the luminosity of total evidence, see Gallow (2019, section 3.1).

and irrelevant influences, and also because of the puzzle it raises. There are generally three positions on how to respond to the puzzle: Higher-Order Defeat/ Calibrationism, Dilemma, and Right Reasons. Each position faces its distinct problems.

In the next several sections, I will defend Calibrationism. I focus on Calibrationism mainly because I think it's the most plausible account of the significance of HOE. It's formally precise, it explains our intuition that one should give up one's original beliefs in typical HOE cases, it generalizes the Higher-Order Defeat view and, as I will argue, the existing objections against it can be successfully addressed.

3 Calibrationism and its Main Motivations

In this section, I clarify some crucial terms in Calibrationism (Section 3.1); I also critically review some of the existing motivations for the typical version of Calibrationism (Section 3.2). My criticism will provide motivation for a new version of Calibrationism; I will defend the new version in later sections.

3.1 Calibrationism

As I have mentioned in Section 1, Calibrationism is a generalization of the claim that HOE defeats the rationality of one's first-order belief. A rough formulation of the view says that one's credence in a proposition p should cohere with one's expected reliability with regard to whether p. And a common, more precise formulation of Calibrationism says:

(i) Bridge
One's credence in a proposition p should match one's expected reliability with regard to p.
(ii) Independence
One's expected reliability with regard to p should be arrived at independently of one's first-order evidence.

Call Calibrationism formulated this way 'Credence-Calibrationism.' For ease of discussion, I will focus mostly on this version of Calibrationism, and I will introduce other versions later when we discuss existing objections against this version, since those other versions are proposed in order to address the objections.[12] *So, up until Section 6, I will use the term 'Calibrationism' to refer to 'Credence-Calibrationism.'*

---

[12] A prominent variation is the so-called Evidential-Calibrationism proposed by Horowitz and Sliwa (2015). Schoenfield (2015) calls Credence-Calibrationism 'J-Calibrationism' and Evidential-Calibrationism 'E-Calibrationism.'

3.1.1 Clarification of Independence: What Exactly Should One Bracket?

Several clarifications of Calibrationism are in order. First, there is a vexing question of how to make Independence more precise. The first thing we should note is that, when we say that one's expected reliability should be formed independently of one's *first-order evidence*, what we mean more exactly is that it should be formed independently of one's *first-order reasoning* from the evidence. As Christensen (2019, p. 17) convincingly argues, a piece of evidence E can bear on a proposition H both in a first-order way (e.g., through bearing worldly connections such as logical, causal, explanatory, or statistical connections to H) and in a higher-order way (through bearing on one's reliability about H), and Independence should only bar relying on reasoning from E to H in a first-order way. For instance, suppose H = [E and 'if F then E'], where F is an arbitrary proposition. Then the reasoning

E; therefore, E;
E; therefore, if F then E,
If both E and [if F then E], then H.
Therefore, if E, then H.

is a piece of first-order reasoning from E to H. But E could also bear on H in the following way

E;

Generally, whenever E is the case, I am unreliable in nonimmediate logical reasoning;
Therefore, I'm unreliable in correctly assessing the connection between E and H.

Independence shouldn't bar relying on E in one's expectation of reliability using this higher-order reasoning. So, strictly speaking, what Independence requires is independence from one's first-order reasoning from E, not independence from the evidence E itself.[13]

But what exactly is the first-order reasoning that one's expectation of reliability should bracket? Does it mean the actual episode of first-order reasoning that one uses when one infers H from E, or does it mean any possible first-order reasoning that one could use to infer H from E? And if one's reasoning consists of several inferential steps, should one bracket the whole reasoning, or only some inferential steps in the reasoning?

---

[13] For this reason, Christensen (2019, p. 17) suggests that, strictly speaking, we should not say that a piece of evidence E is first-order evidence about H; rather, we should say that E is *used* as first-order evidence *in one's reasoning about H*.

I think it's hard to give general answers to these questions. A lot depends on what exactly one's HOE says about one's reliability. For instance, it matters whether the HOE says that one is unreliable in correctly carrying out any possible first-order reasoning from E to H, or whether it only says that one is unreliable in certain kinds of first-order reasoning from E to H. The general point I can make here is this: the exact thing that one's expectation of reliability should bracket should match the exact thing that one's HOE says that one is unreliable at. Since this general point seems to capture the core idea of Independence, I will resist the temptation to make further clarifications. Christensen (2019) provides further details on Independence.

3.1.2 Clarification of 'Expected Reliability'

What exactly is one's 'expected reliability with regard to proposition H'? There are three different answers in the literature. Suppose that one's first-order evidence is E. Then 'expected reliability' could mean:

> *Truth-Reliability*: One's expectation of the objective probability that one forms a correct judgment about H on the basis of E. (Christensen, 2016b; Schoenfield, 2015; Weatherson, n.d.; White, 2009)[14]

> *Direction-Reliability*: One's expectation of the objective probability that one forms a correct judgment about whether E supports H. (Christensen, 2010)

> *Degree-Reliability*: One's expectation of the objective probability that one forms a correct judgment about the exact degree to which E supports H. (Rasmussen et al., 2018)

In all of the three notions, one's expectation of the objective probability of a proposition q is $\sum_x x\mathrm{Cr}$(the objective probability of q is x), where Cr is one's credence function. For instance, if one is 50 percent confident that the objective probability of 'I form a correct judgment about H on the basis of E' is 80 percent, and 50 percent confident that the objective probability is 60 percent, then one's expectation of the objective probability is 70 percent; so, one's expected reliability understood as Truth-Reliability is 70 percent.

We can see that the three notions of expected reliability are different: Truth-Reliability is about reliability in forming a correct judgment on the first-order issue H on the basis of one's first-order evidence, whereas Direction-Reliability and Degree-Reliability is about reliability in getting right the evidential connection between E and H; besides, Degree-Reliability involves a more demanding ability in

---

[14] I follow Weatherson (n.d.) and Schoenfield (2015) in using the term 'judgment' this way: your judgment about p on the basis of E is the proposition among {p, not-p} that you are more confident in on the basis of E.

assessing evidence: one might be reliable in getting the direction of evidential support right, but not reliable in getting the exact degree of support right.

In some of the arguments for or against Calibrationism that I will discuss, advocates of those arguments either use Truth-Reliability, or haven't specified whether they use Truth-Reliability or Direction-Reliability. This conflation between Truth-Reliability and Direction-Reliability is harmless in those cases where the two kinds of reliability happen to match. For instance, in those cases where one is certain that E either entails H or it entails not-H, one can be certain that one correctly judges whether H if and only if one correctly judges whether E entails H, so that one's reliability in correctly judging whether H matches the reliability in correctly judging the evidential support relation. But the two kinds of reliability can come apart, and arguments for or against Calibrationism working with one notion of reliability might not work for those that work with the other kind.

I will work with Truth-Reliability in my following discussion. As I have explained in Section 1.1, evidence about one's reliability in correctly judging the truth of the first-order matter is a more inclusive kind of HOE than evidence about one's reliability in judging the evidential connection. It's more inclusive in the following sense: evidence of unreliability in getting the truth includes but is not limited to evidence of unreliability in getting the evidential relation right. It's true that many times one is unreliable in getting the truth because one is poor at evaluating evidence; but it's certainly not the only reason why one might be unreliable in getting the truth. For instance, one might be fairly reliable in assessing evidential connections but terrible at collecting evidence. Since evidence for this kind of cognitive deficiency will also generate the puzzle explained in Section 1, we'd better include it into our discussion of how to understand the significance of HOE.

There is another reason I want to focus on evidence about one's reliability in correctly judging the truth of the first-order matter, rather than evidence about one's reliability in judging the evidential connection. I think the former kind of evidence is more fundamental in the following sense: the defeating power of the latter kind of evidence seems to derive from the defeating power of the former kind. That is, if we think evidence of unreliability in judging the evidential connection has defeating power, it's probably because we think that unreliability in assessing evidence implies unreliability in getting the truth, and unreliability in getting the truth has defeating power. To put it another way, when I learn that I'm incapable of properly evaluating the evidential connection, the reason that this information gives me pressure to revise my first-order belief lies in that it gives me reason to doubt the likelihood that I form a correct judgment about the first-order matter.

3.2 Main Motivations for Calibrationism

Since Calibrationism consists of two claims (Bridge and Independence), motivations for Calibrationism consist of two parts: those for Bridge and those for Independence. In this section, I will briefly explain the motivation for Independence without going into detailed discussion. (Interested readers should read Christensen's (2019) essay for more detail.) Then I will focus on motivations for Bridge. I will explain two existing motivations for Bridge. I will argue that those motivations fail to establish Bridge, for Bridge requires an *exact match* between our first-order credence and our expected reliability and yet those motivations can't establish such an exact match. This result will be significant for my later argument in Section 6, for I will propose a new version of Calibrationism that doesn't require such an exact match.

3.2.1 The Main Motivation for Independence: Against Bootstrapping Reasoning

The main motivation for Independence is that violating it would lead to dogmatic or bootstrapping reasoning (Christensen, 2011; Elga, 2007). One would be able to reason in the following way: 'E; therefore, H; therefore, E supports H; I believe that E supports H; therefore, my reasoning abilities with regard to whether E supports H is *not* damaged, contrary to what my HOE says; therefore, my HOE must be misleading.' This kind of reasoning sounds problematic, no matter whether one's reasoning from E to H is in fact correct. One way of seeing the oddity of the reasoning is this: in disagreement, this kind of reasoning will not only allow one to dismiss the disagreement with one's intellectual peers, it will also allow one to dismiss the disagreement with one's intellectual superiors.

Calibrationists have given various explanations as to why exactly the bootstrapping reasoning is problematic. Some claim that it manifests bad reasoning dispositions: if one employs the first-order reasoning from E to dismiss HOE when the first-order reasoning is correct, one will be disposed to do the same thing when the reasoning is incorrect (Smithies, 2015). Others claim that your HOE presents you a 'potential defeater,' and a good reasoning from E to H must first respond to such potential defeaters (van Wietmarschen, 2013).[15]

---

[15] For doubts about these and other kinds of motivations for Independence, see Frances (2010), Kelly (2010), Lackey (2010), and Lord (2014). For responses to some of the doubts, see Christensen (2011).

3.2.2 The First Motivation for Bridge: Anti-Akrasia

The main motivation for Bridge is that violating it leads to epistemic akrasia and that epistemic akrasia is irrational. According to a crude formulation of the anti-akrasia requirement, it's irrational to hold a first-order attitude while doubting the rationality of that attitude or the reliability of the underlying cognitive process.

The anti-akrasia requirement has been motivated in several ways. Some think that the requirement is constitutive of the very concept of rationality (Titelbaum, 2015, p. 289). Others argue that akratic doxastic states lead to Moorean-paradoxical assertions of the form 'p, and I shouldn't believe that p' (Huemer, 2011; Smithies, 2012). Still others point out that the normal connection between belief and action is broken when one's belief is akratic: normally, when it's rational for you to have a credence in a proposition, you can act on this credence, say, by accepting certain betting odds on the proposition; but when you think that your credence is irrational or unreliably formed, it's no longer clear that your credence allows you to act accordingly (Horowitz, 2014).

It's worth noting that the anti-akrasia motivation for Bridge is limited in power: it can at best motivate a rough match between credence and expected reliability, but it doesn't motivate an exact match between the two. It might be constitutive of rationality that one shouldn't assign a high credence in p while having low expected reliability, for doing so seems to be 'self-incoherent,' or 'self-undermining.' But it's unclear why it would be self-undermining to be 0.9 confident in p while having 0.8 credence that one correctly judges whether p (where that credence is reached independently of one's first-order reasoning). Moreover, an exact match is not required in order to avoid Moorean paradoxical assertions of the form 'p, but I shouldn't believe p.' When I'm extremely highly confident in p but only slightly less confident in my reliability, I don't have an exact match but I'm still able to avoid Moorean-paradoxical assertions.

You might think that more precise formulations of the anti-akrasia requirement are the so-called Rational-Reflection principles and that such principles do require an exact match between one's credence in p and one's expectation of the rational credence in p (see Elga [2013], Lasonen-Aarnio [2015], and Dorst [2019] for discussion of such principles). However, Rational-Reflection principles are different from Bridge: the former concerns expected rational credence whereas the latter concerns expected reliability, and to say that one's expected rational credence is x is not to say that one's expected reliability concerning whether p is x. So, it's far from clear how such principles support Bridge.

3.2.3 The Second Motivation for Bridge: An Accuracy-Based Argument

The second motivation for Bridge is an accuracy-based argument attributable to Schoenfield (2018). She presents the argument as an argument for Calibrationism (more exactly, for making Calibrationist plans); however, I will argue later in Section 4 that it's at best an argument for Bridge; that is, it cannot be used to motivate Independence. If sound, her argument will show that one's credence should exactly match one's expected reliability. But her argument is unsound, as I will argue below.

Here is Schoenfield's accuracy-based argument. Imagine that you are thinking about making a plan on what credence x to have in a proposition p in the face of getting first-order evidence E and higher-order evidence HOE, and the HOE says that your chance in reaching a correct judgment about p on the basis of E is only 50 percent. Then, in the face of evidence E&HOE, the expected accuracy of making the plan is given by $0.5A(x, 1) + 0.5A(x, 0)$, where $A(x, 1)$ is the accuracy score of having credence x in a truth, and $A(x, 0)$ is the accuracy score of having credence x in a falsehood. Given a widely held requirement that accuracy scores be strictly proper, this quantity is maximized at $x = 0.5$. And this argument can be generalized to those cases where the expected reliability according to the HOE is a value other than 0.5. Thus, your credence in the proposition you judge should exactly match your expected reliability.

This argument for Bridge is unsound. A crucial step in the argument is this: when you are making a plan to hold credence x in the proposition p in the face of getting E and HOE, and when the HOE says that your reliability in reaching a correct judgment is only 50 percent, the expected accuracy of making the plan is given by the following formula:

$$0.5A(x, 1) + 0.5A(x, 0)$$

But this formula is incorrect. The formula assumes that, by making the plan of holding credence x in p in the face of E&HOE (where p happens to your judgment about the issue of whether p on the basis of E), you will assign credence x to all of your judgments regarding whether p. But this assumption is dubious – after all, planning to have credence x in p, where p happens to be your judgment, is *not* planning to have credence x in all of your judgments regarding whether p. Here is an example to explain why Schoenfield's formula assumes that you will assign the same credence x to all of your judgments regarding whether p.

Suppose that you are a meteorologist. Based on your meteorological evidence, you judge that it's raining tomorrow, but then when you look at your track record, you realize that your correctness rate in predicting the weather is only 50 percent. For simplicity, let's imagine that your track record looks like this:

	Your Judgment	The Truth
Day 1	Raining	Raining
Day 2	Raining	Not-Raining
Day 3	Not-Raining	Not-Raining
Day 4	Not-Raining	Raining

That is, only 50 percent of your judgments about whether it will rain are correct. Given this information, how confident should you be in the proposition 'it will rain'? In the accuracy framework, this amounts to the question: what credence in the proposition will maximize expected accuracy?

Now, *if* your credence underlying all of your judgments concerning whether it will rain is the same value x on all days, then Schoenfield's formula will be correct: for 50 percent of the days, you are x confident in the truth; for the other 50 percent of the days, you are x confident in the falsehoods. However, that's a big *if* . Dropping the assumption, Schoenfield's formula will be incorrect. Suppose your credence underlying the judgment 'Raining' is x, but your credence underlying the judgment 'Not-Raining' is y. Then your expected accuracy score will be:

$$a/2A(x, 1) + a/2A(x, 0) + (1 - a)/2A(y, 1) + (1 - a)/2A(y, 0)$$

where a is the ratio of the days of you judging 'Raining' among all days. Clearly, strict propriety of the accuracy measure A will not guarantee that this quantity is maximized when x = 0.5.

So, Schoenfield's formula assumes that you have the same credence underlying your judgment about whether *p*. But there is no reason to think that this assumption is in general correct. Why think that, no matter whether your judgment is *p* or it's not-*p*, the credence underlying that judgment will always be x? Why couldn't you have different credence in the proposition you judge, depending on what you judge? After all, the plan you are making is 'being x confident in *p* in the face of E&HOE,' not 'being x confident in my judgment about *p* in the face of E&HOE, *regardless of what that judgment is.*'

To further explain this point, recall that one's judgment is derived from one's credence. When thinking about what plans to make, one primarily thinks about questions like 'what credence should I have in *p*?' not questions like 'Suppose that I make a judgment about *p*; what credence should I have in *that judgment*?'

So, even if you plan to have credence 0.99 in p, and even if this credence implies that you will judge p, it doesn't mean that by making this plan, you will also have credence 0.99 in not-p every time you judge not-p. To illustrate, let's think about what making a Steadfast plan means. A Steadfast plan says this: match your credence in p with the credence supported by your first-order evidence. There is no reason to think that, if I make this plan, I will assign the same credence to the proposition that I judge regarding whether p, no matter what I judge. What credence I assign to the proposition I judge regarding whether p will depend on what credence in p I think is supported by first-order evidence. If my credence x in p is > 0.5, I will judge p and will be x confident in the proposition I judge, namely, p. If x < 0.5, I will judge not-p and will be 1-x in the proposition I judge. So, to say that I always have the same credence underlying my judgment is to say this: there is a fixed number x that's not 0.5 such that, every time I examine the evidence and make a judgment, either it seems to me that E supports p to degree x, or it seems to me that E supports not-p to degree x. Only this would guarantee that I will have the same credence whatever my judgment about p is. Perhaps some instances of HOE satisfy this condition. But there is no reason to think that this condition holds in all instances of HOE.

In conclusion, Schoenfield's formula for calculating expected accuracy assumes that the relevant judgments mentioned in one's HOE are underwritten by exactly the same level of credence. But we shouldn't think that this assumption holds in general.

To sum up this section, the anti-akrasia motivation for Bridge is plausible but only motivates a rough match, not an exact match, between credence and expected reliability; the accuracy argument can establish an exact match if successful, but the argument rests on a problematic assumption.[16] In the next two sections, I discuss the main problems with Calibrationism.

4 The Problem of Ignoring Evidence

This section discusses a major problem with Calibrationism, the problem that Calibrationism ignores first-order evidence. I explain the problem in Section 4.1. In Section 4.2, I argue that existing solutions to the problem are unsatisfactory.

---

[16] White (2009, p. 239) has raised a different argument for Calibrationism. I will leave it to the readers to figure out what exactly White's argument is and to decide whether it's convincing. (From what I can see, the argument rests on a problematic assumption that's similar to the one that Schoenfield's accuracy argument rests on: it falsely assumes that having credence x in p commits one to having exactly the same credence in judgments about all p-like propositions.)

4.1 Ignoring First-Order Evidence

In Section 2.1, I've mentioned that an important worry faced by Christensen (2010)'s bracketing account of the Higher-Order Defeat view is that it ignores first-order evidence so that rationality comes by too easily. As Kelly (2010) puts it, the basic idea of the worry is that it's very easy to gain HOE, and for many proponents of the Higher-Order Defeat view, there is a simple recipe telling us how to respond to the gained HOE. For example, you can easily gain HOE on a controversial topic by exchanging views with an epistemic peer. And according to many proponents of Conciliationism (which can be regarded the Higher-Order Defeat view applied to cases of peer disagreement), there is a simple recipe of how to respond to the gained HOE: you simply split the difference with your peer. So, even if you start out with an irrational credence relative to your first-order evidence, you can easily adopt the rational credence relative to your total evidence by splitting the difference with a peer who holds a different credence. And in a more dramatic case, two irrational persons will end up with rational credences if they exchange views with each other and split the difference.

Since Calibrationism is a generalization of the Higher-Order Defeat view, and since it commits to an independence principle that requires bracketing first-order reasoning, many scholars have accused Calibrationism of the same problem of ignoring first-order evidence (see Schoenfield [2015] and White [2009]). Calibrationism says that we should match our credence with expected reliability, where the expected reliability calculation is done without consideration of our first-order reasoning. So, what our first-order evidence actually supports is completely dropped out of the picture – what's rational is entirely determined by what our HOE says about our reliability.[17] This means that Calibrationism also faces the problem of making rationality come by too easily: information of expected reliability is easy to come by (basically, you can gain the information just by examining your past track record and seeing how frequently you've believed the truth), and the recommendation of Calibrationism is easy to follow – you simply have the credence matching the expected reliability.

Now, although Kelly's ignoring evidence worry is framed as 'rationality coming by too easily,' I think the real force of his worry doesn't really depend on the fact that HOE is easy to gain and that the recommendation of Calibrationism is easy to follow. The real force of the worry, I take it, is that it's just implausible to say that first-order evidence doesn't matter to rationality.

---

[17] As Schoenfield (2015, p. 431) writes, Calibrationism 'leads to the absurd conclusion that *all* that is required for rational belief is that we match our credences to our expected degree of reliability.'

Suppose your total evidence with regard to p at t_0 is E&HOE, but then at t_1 you gain additional first-order evidence E*, which you recognize as confirming evidence for p. But suppose that your HOE remains the same. (For instance, we can suppose that your HOE implies that your reliability in situations like E is the same as your reliability in situations like E&E*.) Then a view that says that first-order evidence doesn't matter to rationality will imply that your credence in p should remain the same. But this is implausible – after all, you have gained evidence that you recognize as confirming evidence for p, so, intuitively, E&E*&HOE should require a higher credence in p than E&HOE.

To illustrate this point, consider the drug case we discussed in Section 1.4. Imagine that you are a detective deliberating on whether Jack is the murderer. Your evidence includes fingerprints collected from the crime scene and witnesses' testimonies. After carefully analyzing the evidence, you come to believe that the evidence is best explained by Jack being the murderer, and so you judge that Jack is the murderer. Then you receive HOE saying that you are affected by some drug that make people become a random coin-flipper, so that they make correct judgments in this type of case only 50 percent of the time, even though things seem perfectly normal to them. By Calibrationism, your credence in 'Jack is the murderer' should be 0.5. However, suppose that at the next moment, you receive a piece of additional first-order evidence: two more eyewitnesses independently claim that they saw Jack at the crime scene. This evidence clearly supports the case for Jack being the murderer. But suppose that your higher-order evidence remains the same: it still says that you are effectively a random coin-flipper and your expected reliability is 50 percent. Calibrationism says that your credence in Jack being the murderer should be the same. But this seems implausible – it seems that with the additional witnesses' testimonies, your credence should increase.

Calibrationists have offered various responses to the problem of ignoring evidence. In what follows, I review two existing responses and I argue that both are unsuccessful. Some of the objections discussed are not new.

4.2 The First Response: Calibrationism Doesn't Allow Ignoring Evidence

The first kind of response acknowledges that the implication of ignoring first-order evidence is problematic, and it seeks to revise Calibrationism so that it doesn't have the implication. Calibrationists have offered two different revisions to achieve this purpose.

4.2.1 Weakening Calibrationism

The first revision is to weaken Calibrationism. One might say that obeying Calibrationism is only a necessary condition of rationality, not a sufficient one, and that what our first-order evidence supports also matters. A suggestion along this line is given by Christensen in response to Kelly's worry that Conciliationism ignores first-order evidence:

> Conciliationism tells us what the proper response is to one particular kind of evidence. . . . But having taken correct account of one bit of evidence cannot be equivalent to having beliefs that are (even propositionally) rational, all things considered. If one starts out by botching things epistemically, and then takes correct account of one bit of evidence, it's unlikely that one will end up with fully rational beliefs. (Christensen, 2011, p. 4)

So, according to Christensen (2011), Conciliationism is only a view about how to rationally respond to the evidence provided by peer disagreement, and rationally responding to this single piece of evidence doesn't imply rationally responding to one's *total* evidence; moreover, for one to rationally respond to one's total evidence, one's initial belief before gaining the disagreement evidence must also be rational.

Extending this response to Calibrationism, we can say that calibrating one's credence to expected reliability is only a necessary condition of rationality since it's only a view about how to respond to HOE, and for one's credence to be rational relative to one's total evidence, one's credence before gaining the HOE must also be rational; that is, one's initial credence must be rational relative to one's first-order evidence.

As Schoenfield (2015, pp. 437–44) points out, the above weakened version of Calibrationism faces a serious problem: it creates epistemic dilemmas in those cases where intuitively there are no dilemmas. Consider this case: an oracle tells one that one's reliability degree with regard to whether p is 0 percent; that is, one is perfectly anti-reliable with regard to whether p. Suppose that, before gaining this HOE, one originally judges that p and one's credence in p is *irrational* relative to one's first-order evidence. Then when one gains the HOE, what should one do according to this weakened version of Calibrationism? If one calibrates to the expected reliability, one will not end up with a credence that's rational relative to the total evidence, since one doesn't start out with the credence rational relative to the first-order evidence; but if one doesn't calibrate, one will also not end up with a rational credence, since calibration is a necessary condition of rationality. So, the weakened version of Calibrationism says that one faces an epistemic dilemma. But intuitively, one doesn't face any dilemma at all, because there seems to be a perfectly rational response: if one originally judges that p and if the oracle says that one is perfectly anti-reliable in judging whether p, it seems that decreasing credence in p to 0 will be a perfectly rational response.[18]

Here is another attempt to avoid the problem of ignoring evidence, which is also in the spirit of weakening Calibrationism. A Calibrationist can appeal to the distinction made by Staffel between transitional attitudes and terminal attitudes, and he can claim that Calibrationism is only about what transitional attitudes are rational. According to Staffel (in press, p. 7), transitional attitudes are attitudes that 'agents hold towards the answers to specific questions before they have, by their own lights, finished deliberating about how the evidence they currently have bears on these questions,' while terminal attitudes are attitudes that agents hold when they think that they have 'finished' the deliberation, so that a further, better deliberation on evidence won't change their opinion. In discussing how to respond to HOE provided by peer disagreement, Staffel suggests that we can understand Conciliationism as a view about what transitional attitudes are rational and Steadfastness as a view about what terminal attitudes are rational. For instance, she suggests that in the classic restaurant bill example that motivates Conciliationism, suspending judgment is only a rational transitional attitude, since the agents know that if they deliberate on their evidence better by rechecking their original reasoning, they will not suspend judgment.

Now, I find Staffel's account plausible in dealing with the negative, potentially defeating kind of HOE, but not so plausible in dealing with the positive kind of HOE. In the restaurant case, it's plausible to say that one should suspend judgment but should also think that this attitude is only temporary. Similarly, if one is originally 0.8 confident in a proposition p but then receives HOE saying that one is affected by a drug so that one's reliability is only 50 percent, a Calibrationist may say that credence 0.5 is only a rational transitional attitude, since one should think 'if I can deliberate on my evidence better, say, if I deliberate again after the drug effect has gone, I probably won't hold a 0.5 credence.' But suppose the HOE says that one's reliability degree is 95 percent, not 50 percent, and suppose that one obeys Calibrationism by revising one's credence to 0.95. Should one think 'if I can deliberate better, I probably won't hold a 0.95 credence'? The answer is negative. After all, the HOE says that one doesn't suffer any cognitive deficiency in evidence-deliberation at all; quite the contrary – the HOE says that one is doing quite well. (Note that we shouldn't think that any reliability degree below 100 percent marks some cognitive deficiencies. When evidence is fallible, even an ideal reasoner will not reach 100 percent reliability in forming correct judgments on the basis of the evidence.)

---

[18] For further worries about this weakened version of Calibrationism, see Tal (2021, pp. 52–56).

Therefore, it's hard to maintain that credence 0.95 is only a rational transitional attitude.

4.2.2 Strengthening Calibrationism

The second revision is opposite to the first one: rather than weakening Calibrationism to get rid of the problematic implication of ignoring first-order evidence, we strengthen Calibrationism by incorporating first-order evidence. With such a revision, it's now much harder to follow Calibrationism. For instance, Horowitz and Sliwa (2015) defend a version of Calibrationism that's called 'Evidential Calibrationism,' which requires that we calibrate the judgment *that's supported by first-order evidence*, not the judgment we happen to hold, to expected reliability. So, if one judges that p while one's first-order evidence actually supports not-p, then one should match one's credence in not-p, rather than one's credence in p, to expected reliability.

Evidential Calibrationism is a promising attempt at incorporating first-order evidence into a Calibrationist framework. However, it suffers two clear problems. First, it faces a problem of motivation. Since expected reliability is defined as reliability of one's own judgment, not the judgment that's actually supported by one's first-order evidence, it's mysterious why one should calibrate one's credence in the judgment supported by first-order evidence, rather than one's own judgment, to the expected reliability. Second, Evidential Calibrationism only incorporates the *direction* of first-order evidence, but it still ignores its *strength* (White, 2009, p. 240). Imagine two persons with first-order evidence that agrees in direction but differs in strength – one person's first-order evidence supports p to degree 0.9 while the other's first-order evidence only supports p to degree 0.6 – and suppose that their expected reliability is both 0.8. Then, Evidential Calibrationism says that their credence in p should both be 0.8. So, it implies that the strength of their first-order evidence doesn't matter to rational credence. The worry of ignoring evidence remains.

4.3 The Second Response: Sometimes We Should Ignore Evidence

The second kind of response is to admit that Calibrationism allows ignoring evidence but maintain that sometimes ignoring evidence is exactly the right thing to do. For example, Steel (2018) argues that, when you antecedently expect that responding to your first-order evidence has only 50 percent chance of reaching a correct judgment, setting your credence to 50 percent no matter what the first-order evidence actually supports is exactly the right thing to do. To support this claim, Steel gives an accuracy argument: when accuracy scores are strictly proper, matching credence with expected reliability maximizes expected accuracy. Schoenfield (2018) gives a similar accuracy argument.

In Section 3, I have argued that the accuracy argument is problematic even if we just view it as a motivation for Bridge. Here, I present two additional worries when we view it as an argument for Calibrationism (which commits to both Bridge and Independence). First, the argument looks circular, since the proof that the argument rests on must assume Independence.

To see why, recall Schoenfield's proof. Imagine that you are thinking about making a plan to have credence x in p in the face of first-order evidence E and higher-order evidence HOE, and the HOE says that your reliability in reaching a correct judgment on p is only 50 percent. According to Schoenfield, the expected accuracy of making the plan is given by

$$0.5A(x, 1) + 0.5A(x, 0)$$

where $A(x, 1)$ is the accuracy score of having credence x in a truth, and $A(x, 0)$ is the accuracy score of having credence x in a falsehood. Assuming that accuracy scores must be strictly proper, this quantity is maximized at x = 0.5.

This accuracy argument fails to support Calibrationism, because it has smuggled in the Calibrationist commitment of Independence. For why think that the expected accuracy of the plan is given by $0.5A(x, 1) + 0.5A(x, 0)$? Why think that, if you make the plan, you will form a correct judgment only 50 percent of the time? Of course, this is what your HOE tells you. But why listen only to what HOE says about your reliability? To insist that you should only listen to HOE about your reliability is to presuppose Independence, which says that you should bracket first-order evidence E in assessing your reliability. For if you could rely on E in assessing the reliability of your judgment, then you should think that when planning to have credence x in p, you will form a correct judgment 100x percent of the time, not 50 percent of the time: suppose that from E you will judge p (the case where you will judge not-p is similar); then you will know that you will judge p, and thus you will know 'I form a correct judgment about p iff p,' which means that your credence in forming a correct judgment about p will be the same as your credence in p. If so, your expected accuracy of the plan will not be given by $0.5A(x, 1) + 0.5A(x, 0)$ but by

$$xA(x, 1) + (1 - x)A(x, 0)$$

and there is no reason to think that this quantity is maximized at x = 0.5.

So, the expected-accuracy argument for Calibrationist planning is circular because it has to assume Independence, a core commitment of Calibrationism. In fact, I suspect that the problem of circularity will arise for *any* potential expected-accuracy argument for Calibrationism. To calculate the expected accuracy of a plan about how to respond to first-order evidence E and higher-order evidence HOE, we must first answer the question: from *which perspective* are we viewing the expected accuracy? Is it the perspective given by HOE or the perspective given by E? But to answer this question is already to take a stance on Independence. So, no expected-accuracy argument can provide noncircular support for Independence. Since it's the Calibrationist's commitment to Independence that leads to the result of ignoring first-order evidence, no expected-accuracy argument can provide noncircular support for the claim that we should ignore first-order evidence in the face of HOE.

My second worry about the accuracy argument for ignoring first-order evidence is that it seems to prove too much. The accuracy argument generalizes to those cases where the expected reliability is not 0.5. So, even if your expected reliability is a much higher value, say, 0.9, the accuracy argument will still say that you should ignore first-order evidence and should just calibrate credence in your judgment to 0.9. But this is counterintuitive. It's indeed plausible to say that, when your expected reliability is 0.5 or lower, you should ignore first-order evidence – it's reasonable to bracket that evidence when the objective probability that you form correct judgments on the basis of the evidence is low. But why think that you should still ignore evidence when that probability is much higher? It seems that, when the risk of incorrectly using that evidence is small, the risk is worth taking for the potential benefit brought by basing credence on a larger body of evidence.

To sum up, in this section, I have explained the alleged problem that Calibrationism ignores evidence, and I have argued that the existing responses to this problem are all unsatisfactory.[19] In the next section, we move on to another major problem with Calibrationism.

5 The Conflict with Conditionalization

The Bayesian norm of conditionalization says that, when getting new evidence, one's new credence in a proposition should match one's old credence conditional on the evidence. This norm is widely taken to be a rational way of updating credence.

---

[19] There is a response to the problem different from the ones discussed. In defending a principle that he calls 'Top-Down Guidance,' which says that one should have the credence that matches one's expectation of the credence supported by one's first-order evidence, Skipper (2021, pp. 11572–73) says that this principle doesn't ignore first-order evidence, since it requires one to treat the HOE about what one's first-order evidence supports as a guide about what one's first-order evidence supports.

I think this response is not very helpful to the Calibrationist, since Calibrationism is mainly concerned with how to respond to HOE about one's reliability, not how to respond to HOE about what one's first-order evidence supports. As I've explained in the drug case, evidence that one is unreliable because one is effectively a random coin-flipper offers no guidance on what one's first-order evidence supports.

This section discusses another major problem with Calibrationism, the problem that Calibrationism conflicts with conditionalization. I discuss two different arguments for the claim that there is such a conflict, the first one due to Christensen (2010) and the second one due to White (2009). I argue in Section 5.1 that Christensen's argument can be blocked. Then, I present White's argument in Section 5.2, and admit that it constitutes a serious challenge against Calibrationism. I discuss how White's challenge can be met in the next section.

Before discussing Christensen's and White's arguments, I'll mention one early Bayesian argument against Conciliationism just to set it aside. In the peer disagreement literature, some scholars have argued that the view of splitting-the-difference doesn't sit well with Bayesianism (Fitelson & Jehle, 2009; Shogenji, 2007). Since Calibrationism implies Conciliationism, which was once widely taken to be associated with splitting-the-difference, the Bayesian troubles for splitting-the-difference might also be viewed as troubles for Calibrationism. Roughly, one trouble is that splitting-the-difference fails to preserve probabilistic independence: two persons who disagree on p and on q and yet agree that p and q are independent no longer think that the two propositions are independent after splitting the difference. Another trouble is that splitting-the-difference doesn't commute with conditionalization; that is, splitting-and-then-conditionalizing can result in a credence that's different from conditionalizing-and-then-splitting (Loewer & Laddaga, 1985).

I will set aside the above Bayesian troubles: since splitting-the-difference is only one reading of Conciliationism, perhaps Conciliationists can avoid those troubles by distancing themselves from splitting-the-difference. In fact, it's an increasing trend among Conciliationists to distance themselves from the simple view that we should always split the difference in the face of peer disagreement.

Now turn to the alleged problem that Calibrationism conflicts with conditionalization. There are two arguments for the existence of the conflict. The first argument, due to Christensen (2010), is more ambitious: it says that *any* rational person cannot satisfy both Calibrationism and conditionalization. The second argument, due to White (2009), is more modest: it says that a rational person can satisfy both norms *only in very special cases*; say, only when the person's priors take certain specific values.

About Christensen's argument for the conflict, I defend a response that's been briefly suggested by Christensen himself, which says that the argument will not go through if we understand updating on HOE as updating on self-locating information. About White's argument, I claim that the alleged conflict with conditionalization doesn't undermine the spirit of Calibrationism but only speaks to its poor formulation. I propose a new version of Calibrationism in the next section and then argue that it can avoid the conflict with conditionalization.

5.1 Christensen's Argument That Calibrationism Conflicts with Conditionalization

Recall the drug example mentioned in Section 1.1. Let E refer to my first-order evidence, and let's suppose that E supports H to a high degree. My HOE is evidence that I've been given a drug that impairs one's abilities in assessing the evidential bearing of evidence E on H. The original characterization of this HOE doesn't specify when I'm drugged. Now, let's suppose that the current time is Monday and the HOE is evidence that *I'm drugged on Monday*. Let C_0 refer to the earlier credence I held on Sunday, when my total evidence doesn't include E&HOE yet, and let C_1 refer to the credence I hold now on Monday. Calibrationists claim

(1) $C_1(H) = C_1(H/E\&HOE) = LOW$

However, Calibrationists must also accept

(2) $C_0(H/E\&HOE) = C_0(H/E) = HIGH$

This is because the HOE only says that my cognitive ability is impaired on Monday, which means that on Sunday I should not worry about my cognitive abilities; moreover, on Sunday, I should regard my impaired abilities on Monday as irrelevant to the truth of H. But (1) and (2) show that I must violate conditionalization, since by stipulation, E&HOE is all the new information I gain from Sunday to Monday.[20]

What gives rise to the conflict? Here is an answer. As we've said, an important feature of HOE is that it seems to have no bearing on the truth of one's first-order belief; so, there must be a perspective from which you know that your HOE has this feature, a perspective that's described by a credence function you hold at some time – that is what statement (2) says. And yet when you gain such HOE, Calibrationism says that you must listen to it by reducing to your credence, that is, you must now regard the HOE as relevant to the truth of your first-order belief after all, and this is what statement (1) says. So, gaining HOE seems to require you to disregard your prior interpretation of the significance of HOE and thus require you to violate conditionalization.

---

[20] A Bayesian will say that (1) alone is already a violation of Bayesian norms (in particular, the norm of logical omniscience) in those cases where E is entailing evidence for H (see Christensen [2007]). However, this challenge is not a fatal one: Calibrationists can avail themselves of the multiple ways that Bayesians have proposed to relax the logical omniscience requirement. See Skipper and Bjerring (2020) and the references therein.

5.2 The Self-Location Strategy

Christensen (2010, p. 201) has briefly suggested a way of avoiding the above conflict with conditionalization: we should understand updating on HOE as updating on self-locating information. Here, I won't give a full defense of this self-location strategy; I will largely play defensive, by arguing that an important objection that's been pressed against this strategy fails.

What's the self-location strategy? One way of putting it is to say that the HOE is ill-characterized; instead of saying 'I'm drugged *on Monday*,' it should be characterized as the self-locating information 'I'm drugged *now*.' If so, then the Calibrationist can claim that $C_0(H/E\&HOE)$ should be low, not high. 'I'm drugged on Monday' shouldn't worry me when I assess E on Sunday, but 'I'm drugged *now*' should. Another way of fleshing out the self-location strategy is to deny that E&HOE is all the evidence I gain. For on Sunday I don't know *it's Monday now*, but for (1) to be true, I must know on Monday *it's Monday now*; otherwise knowing that I'm drugged on Monday shouldn't worry me on Monday. Therefore, I must have also gained the self-locating information *it's Monday now*. In other words, what worries me on Monday is not the non-self-locating information 'I'm drugged on Monday,' but the self-locating information 'I'm drugged on Monday *and* it's Monday now.'

Schoenfield (2018) has pressed an important objection against this self-location strategy. She objects that this move reconciles Calibrationism with conditionalization only at the cost of losing the main motivation of obeying conditionalization in the first place. We want to obey conditionalization because it maximizes expected accuracy. However, conditionalization maximizes expected accuracy only when certain crucial assumption is satisfied. But the problem is that, if HOE were characterized as self-locating information, then that crucial assumption will *not* be satisfied when we have HOE. So, conditionalizing on HOE, when the HOE is characterized as self-locating information, will *not* maximize expected accuracy.

This is the first stage of her argument. In the second stage, she discusses what updating procedure maximizes expected accuracy when the crucial assumption in question is not satisfied. She argues that a generalization of conditionalization, which she calls conditionalization*, is such a procedure. But she argues that if we apply conditionalization* to HOE, we would get a Steadfastness result, not a Calibrationist result; that is, $C_1(H)$ should be high, not low.[21] In sum, her objection to the self-location strategy consists of two claims:

---

[21] I should note that Schoenfield (2018) endorses Calibrationism despite this result – she makes a distinction between rational plans to conform to and rational plans to make, and she argues that although Calibrationism is not a rational plan to conform to, it's a rational plan to make.

(i) If HOE is characterized as self-locating information, then conditionalizing on HOE will lead to a Calibrationist result, but it will not maximize expected accuracy;

(ii) A more general norm of updating, conditionalization*, will maximize expected accuracy, but it will not lead to a Calibrationist result when applied to HOE.

Schoenfield's argument for (ii) has already been criticized, on the ground that it's questionable whether conditionalization* is really a correct generalization of conditionalization (Bradley, 2020a). But her argument for (i), if successful, will still harm the Calibrationists. Here I will argue that her argument for (i) is also unsuccessful.

As I've mentioned, Schoenfield's reason for (i) rests on the claim that certain crucial assumption must be in place for conditionalization to maximize expected accuracy. If we look at Greaves and Wallace's (2006) proof that conditionalization maximizes expected accuracy, we can see that the assumption is certain transparency condition about one's evidence:

> Factivity:
> For the conditionalization plan on the evidence partition {Ei} to maximize expected accuracy according to one's credence function C_0, {Ei} must satisfy this condition: for any element Ei in this partition, one is certain 'one learns Ei only if Ei is true.'

As Schoenfield points out, this statement is not very clear when it comes to updating on self-locating information. If Ei is a self-locating proposition that changes truth-value over time, then when we say, 'One learns Ei only if Ei is true,' do we mean 'Ei is true at the time before one learns Ei' or 'Ei is true at the time one learns Ei'? Schoenfield maintains that it should be the former. Let's call that earlier time t_0 and the latter time when Ei is learned t_1. So, she claims that the condition in Factivity should be generalized into

> Factivity-indexed
> For any element Ei in the evidence partition {Ei}, one is certain at t_0 'one learns Ei at t_1 only if Ei is true at t_0.'

Then Schoenfield argues that, if HOE is characterized as the self-locating information 'I'm drugged now,' Factivity-indexed is not satisfied. On Sunday, I don't think [I gain evidence 'I'm drugged now' on Monday only if 'I'm drugged now' is true on Sunday]. So, Schoenfield concludes that, if HOE is characterized as self-locating information, then conditionalizing on HOE doesn't maximize expected accuracy.

This argument is fallacious: Factivity-indexed is not a correct generalization of Factivity to cases of self-locating information. I claim that the relevant time should be t_1, not t_0; that is, the correct generalization should be:

Factivity-indexed*
For any element Ei in the evidence partition {Ei}, one is certain at t_0 'one learns Ei at t_1 only if Ei is true at t_1.'

At the first sight, you might agree with Schoenfield that the relevant time should obviously be the earlier time t_0. For the notion 'expected accuracy' is expectation relative to one's earlier credence function C_0, not expectation relative to one's latter credence C_1. Suppose that I plan to follow conditionalization; in particular, suppose that I plan to set my credence in Ei to certainty if I later learn Ei. Then it might seem obvious that I want that, if I later learn Ei, then Ei is true at the earlier time. Only this would guarantee that, from the earlier perspective, becoming certain of Ei will result in certainty in a truth.

But this reasoning is fallacious. If Ei changes truth-value, then I don't want my later credence to match what's true *now*; rather, I want it to match what's true *at the later time when I gain Ei*. This is so even if I'm evaluating expected accuracy from my earlier perspective. For the notion of accuracy essentially measures the degree of match between a doxastic state and the external world, and even from my earlier perspective, the relevant world state we aspire to match should be the world state *at the time at which the doxastic state is held*, not the world state at the earlier time. So, for a proposition E, if I know that I will become certain of E at t_1 when I learn E at t_1, I want it to be the case that E is true *at t_1* when I learn E at t_1. Only this can guarantee that my later credence in E at t_1 matches what-the-world-is-like-at-t_1.[22]

So, Factivity should be understood as Factivity-indexed* rather than Factivity-indexed. If I'm correct, then two things follow. First, there is no reason to think that conditionalizing on HOE, where the HOE is understood as self-locating information, will fail to maximize expected accuracy. For it's reasonable to assume that the condition stated in Factivity-indexed* is satisfied; that is, it's reasonable to assume that I can be certain on Sunday [I gain evidence 'I'm drugged now' on Monday only if 'I'm drugged now' is true on Monday] – this is simply the assumption that I'm certain on Sunday that my source of information

---

[22] Then what's wrong the example that Schoenfield (2018, p. 703) uses to motivate Facitivity-indexed? Here is my diagnosis: the element in the evidence partition {Ei} should be about the *strongest* proposition one might learn, and yet in the example, the supposition 'Taylor's is open today' is not the strongest proposition one might learn. The example assumes that I will know it's Monday when it's Monday. So, the supposition should be the conjunction 'Taylor's open today and it's Monday today.'

as to whether I'm drugged is a reliable one, so that I won't be fed false evidence on Monday as to whether I'm drugged.

Second, there is also no reason to think that conditionalization won't maximize expected accuracy in some paradigmatic cases of self-locating information. For instance, suppose that I stare at the clock and watch the hand going from '2:00' to '2:01.' The required condition stated in Factivity-indexed* is satisfied, since I'm certain at 2:00 [I gain evidence 'it's 2:01 now' at 2:01 only if 'it's 2:01 now' is true at 2:01] (I'm certain of this conditional since the consequent is a trivial truth.) And applying conditionalization indeed gives us the right result here: I should become certain 'it's 2:01 now' once I gain evidence 'it's 2:01 now.'

To conclude, there is no reason to think that if HOE is characterized as self-locating information, then conditionalizing on HOE will not maximize expected accuracy. The self-location strategy is safe.

5.3 White's Argument That Calibrationism Conflicts with Conditionalization

Now, let's turn to White's (2009) argument that Calibrationism conflicts with conditionalization. This argument attempts to show that a rational person can satisfy both norms only in very special cases, more exactly, only when the person's prior takes certain specific value. Informally, his argument is that Calibrationism requires us to treat ourselves as instruments like medical devices or thermometers, and that Calibrationism has committed something like 'the base-rate fallacy,' a type of fallacy that people often make in updating credences upon learning the judgment of an instrument. A common example of this fallacy is this: when a person learns that a highly reliable medical device says that she has lung cancer, she becomes highly confident that she has lung cancer, ignoring how rare lung cancer is among the general population. According to Bayesianism, the person's reasoning is fallacious: if proposition p has a low prior, then even if a highly reliable instrument says that p, one's posterior credence after conditionalizing on the instrument's judgment might still be low. In general, conditionalization implies that when the reliability degree of the instrument is r, you should have credence r in the judgment made by the instrument only in the special cases where your prior is 0.5.

Here is a reconstruction of White's formal argument. Suppose that your current total evidence about H includes: first-order evidence E, psychological evidence 'I judge that H,' and HOE that implies that your expected reliability is r. Calibrationism says that your credence in H should be r. Let C_1 refer to your current credence, and let $C_{HOE\&E}$ refer to the credence you held before learning 'I judge H.' By conditionalization,

$$C_1(H) = C_{HOE \& E}(H/I \text{ judge } H)$$
$$= C_{HOE \& E}(I \text{ judge } H/H)C_{HOE \& E}(H)/C_{HOE \& E}(I \text{ judge } H/H)$$
$$C_{HOE \& E}(H) + C_{HOE \& E}(I \text{ judge } H/\text{not-H}) \, C_{HOE \& E}(\text{not-H})$$
$$= r \, \& \, C_{HOE \& E}(H)/r \, \& \, C_{HOE \& E}(H) + (1\text{-}r)C_{HOE \& E}(\text{not-H})$$
$$= r \text{ iff } C_{HOE \& E}(H) = 0.5$$

So, when your expected reliability is r, you should have credence r in H only if, before you learn that you judge H, your credence in H was 0.5. But this cannot be the case: assuming that you only learn the truth, if you learn that you judge H, your credence in H before the learning must certainly be higher than 0.5 (recall that you judge H just in case you are more confident in H than in not-H on the basis of E).

Here, the Calibrationist can push back this way: this reasoning assumes that there is a moment where you have E and you judge H on the basis of E, but you are uncertain that you judge H and only learn 'I judge H' at a later time. But this is impossible, because once a rational agent has E, she forms a high credence in H and has judgment H (because we have supposed that E supports H), and rational agents are certain of what their credence is at the moment they form the credence.

But White's argument could be reformulated to avoid this problem. Let C_0 be a rational initial prior – i.e., a rational credence function with no evidence. Then the Calibrationist accepts

$$C_0(H/E \, \& \, HOE \, \& \, I \text{ judge } H) = C_0(H/HOE \, \& \, I \text{ judge } H)$$

This is because the Calibrationist thinks that, when your total evidence is E&HOE&[I judge H], your credence in H is entirely determined by what HOE says about the reliability of your judgment, and the first-order evidence E doesn't make a difference; that is, when you have HOE, your judgment screens off your first-order evidence E. If so, the Calibrationist must accept

$$C_1(H) = C_0(H/E \, \& \, HOE \, \& \, I \text{ judge } H)$$
$$= C_0(H/HOE \, \& \, I \text{ judge } H)$$
$$= C_0(I \text{ judge } H/H \, \& \, HOE)C_0(H/HOE)/C_0(I \text{ judge } H/H \, \& \, HOE)$$
$$C_0(H/HOE) + C_0(I \text{ judge } H/\text{not-H} \, \& \, HOE)C_0(\text{not-H}/HOE)$$
$$= r \, \& \, C_0(H/HOE)/r \, \& \, C_0(H/HOE) + (1\text{-}r)C_0(\text{not-H}/HOE)$$
$$= r \text{ iff } C_0(H/HOE) = 0.5$$

But since HOE by itself is not evidence relevant to H, we have $C_0(H/HOE) = C_0(H)$. Therefore, the Calibrationist must accept

$$C_1(H) = r \text{ iff } C_0(H) = 0.5$$

And since the Calibrationist thinks that $C_1(H) = r$, he must think $C_0(H) = 0.5$.

But it's clearly probabilistically incoherent if your initial priors in *all* propositions are 0.5. (Here is one way to see this: if you are probabilistically coherent then $C_0(H) = C_0(H \& Q) + C_0(H \& \text{not-Q})$, where Q is an arbitrary proposition. Then it's impossible that $C_0(H)$, $C_0(H \& Q)$, and $C_0(H \& \text{not-Q})$ are all 0.5.) The upshot is that you can obey both Calibrationism and conditionalization *only* in those cases where your initial prior credence in the proposition in question is 0.5.[23]

This is a serious problem for Calibrationism. However, I will argue that White's argument doesn't undermine the core spirit of Calibrationism, but only speaks to its ill formulation. In Section 6, I will propose a new version of Calibrationism and argue that it avoids the conflict with conditionalization. But before that, let's see if the Calibrationist can just accept the conflict.

5.4 Should Calibrationists Just Accept the Conflict with Conditionalization?

Perhaps Calibrationists can say that we should just accept the conflict with conditionalization. Unlike the self-location strategy, which aims to avoid the conflict, this new response admits the conflict but insists that the conflict is to be expected and allowed, because violating conditionalization is exactly the right thing to do in HOE cases. This new response that we should allow the conflict can be fleshed out in two different ways. I will argue that both ways are unconvincing.

Here is how the first way goes. Conditionalization essentially asks our later self to cohere with our earlier self; more specifically, it asks our later self's interpretation of evidence to agree with our earlier self's.[24] In Levi's (1980) terms, it demands that we don't change our 'confirmational commitments.' This demand may be reasonable in normal situations where you have no reason to change your confirmational commitments, so that the default position is to trust your earlier self. But in HOE cases, gaining HOE should make you doubt your earlier self's interpretation of evidence (assuming that the HOE takes the form 'you've been drugged all along so that your earlier self is also cognitively impaired.') So, it's not surprising that accommodating HOE requires violating conditionalization.

---

[23] Isaacs (2021) raises a similar objection against Calibrationism: in requiring us to set our credence to expected reliability, the Calibrationist has committed the base-rate fallacy because it forgets the influence of the prior.

[24] Conditionalization presupposes a principle that's called 'rigidity,' which says that gaining evidence E (and nothing else) shouldn't change one's conditional probability C(H/E), for any H.

This way of justifying violating conditionalization is problematic. When we claim that conditionalization requires you to preserve your earlier self's interpretation of evidence, the claim comes with an important caveat: the evidence in question must be all the evidence you have gained between the two times. That is, what conditionalization requires is that gaining E *and nothing else* shouldn't change your conditional probability H/E. But in HOE cases, you have also gained HOE at the latter time. So, even if accommodating HOE means that $C_1(H/E)$ differs from $C_0(H/E)$, it doesn't mean you have violated conditionalization.

Perhaps proponents of this way of justifying accepting the conflict with conditionalization don't mean to say that gaining HOE changes your interpretation of E; rather, what they mean is that gaining HOE changes your interpretation of E&HOE. But it's unclear why Calibrationists should say so. After all, your HOE says that your capacity in assessing your *first-order evidence* has impaired; it doesn't say that your capacity in assessing your *total evidence*, which includes both your first-order evidence E and your HOE, has impaired. Therefore, it's unclear why gaining HOE means that you should change your interpretation of E&HOE.

Here is a second way of fleshing out the response that violating conditionalization is exactly the right thing to do when one gains HOE: gaining HOE has the same effect as losing information, since it requires you to bracket evidence; but when one loses information, we all accept that violating conditionalization is exactly the right thing to do (Bradley, 2020b; Levinstein, n.d.). For instance, at noon you might be certain that you've had noodles for lunch, given your fresh memory of having noodles for lunch at noon, but as the time moves to dusk you might lose this memory and thus become uncertain that you had noodles for lunch. This loss of certainty violates conditionalization (since conditionalization requires preserving certainties) but is exactly the right thing to do.

It's certainly attractive to model Higher-Order Defeat as information loss: being required to bracket your evidence E when considering your opinion on H is indeed similar to losing E as evidence. However, this apparent analogy should be resisted. Intuitively, Higher-Order Defeat and information loss are importantly different phenomenon: you are not bracketing E in *all reasoning, but merely* bracketing E in your *first-order reasoning about H* – after all, the bracketing still allows you to be certain of E, to rely on E in *higher-order reasoning* about H (see the distinction between first-order reasoning from E and higher-order reasoning from E in Section 3.1.1), and to rely on E in reasoning about *other propositions that are not related to H*, whereas all these things are not allowed if you lose E as evidence.

Here is a more serious problem with the information-loss strategy of justifying violating conditionalization: the strategy doesn't sit comfortably with a full-blown Calibrationist position that demands Calibrationist *planning*. Admittedly, Calibrationism in our original formulation is a view about how to respond to HOE when you actually gain HOE, not about how to plan in the event of gaining HOE, before you gain HOE. However, I take it that a full-blown Calibrationist should want to say not only that calibration is the right response to HOE when you gain HOE, but also that, in making plans before you gain HOE, you should *plan* to calibrate in the event of gaining HOE. (Here is an analogy: a full-blown advocate of conditionalization should not only say that you should conditionalize upon gaining new evidence, but also that you should plan to do so before you gain new evidence, if you are making plans about how to update credence.)

The problem is that, if Higher-Order Defeat is modeled as information loss, then you shouldn't *plan to calibrate*, even if you should calibrate at the moment of gaining HOE. To see why, note that, even if a credence C_1 is rational when one actually loses information, one shouldn't *plan* to adopt C_1 in the event of losing information. For instance, even if you should become uncertain that you had noodles for lunch when you lose memory at dusk, you shouldn't make this plan at noon:

> If I lose memory at dusk about what I had for lunch, be uncertain at dusk in the proposition 'I had noodles for lunch.'

The reason is that this plan doesn't maximize expected accuracy; more exactly, it doesn't maximize expected accuracy *when the expectation is taken by the relevant credence function*. To clarify, let's suppose that your current evidence is E, and you are making plans about what to do if you lose part of E, say, evidence E*, at the next moment. We all agree that, at the next moment, you should become uncertain that E*. But from your current point of view, a view in which E* is true, being uncertain in E* has less expected accuracy than keeping certainty in E*. And when we make plans about what to do in the event of losing evidence, your current perspective, rather than your later impoverished perspective, should be the relevant credence by which expectation is taken. So, you shouldn't make such a plan:

If I *lose* evidence E*, become uncertain in E*.

So, cases of information loss have the peculiar feature that you shouldn't plan to adopt the attitude that's rational at the moment of information loss. Therefore, if a Calibrationist models Higher-Order Defeat as information loss, she will have to say that you shouldn't plan to adopt the attitude that's rational at the moment of gaining HOE; that is, you shouldn't plan to calibrate. This is unacceptable to a full-blown Calibrationist.

This points to a deeper problem with the information loss strategy. Information loss (such as forgetting) is a bad thing, and we should take measures to avoid it if we can. If rational response to HOE is modeled as information loss, then gaining HOE is a bad thing, and we should take measures to avoid HOE if we can. But this is not how a Calibrationist should think about HOE. Intuitively, gaining HOE is not a bad thing. Quite the contrary, it seems that we fallible agents should seek information about our reliability; at the very least, we should not take measures to avoid such information. For instance, we shouldn't avoid talking to those peers who might disagree with us.

To conclude this section, Christensen's argument that Calibrationism conflicts with conditionalization doesn't work if HOE is understood as self-locating information, and Schoenfield's objection against this strategy is flawed. White's argument for the conflict is more serious, and the Calibrationist shouldn't just accept the conflict. In the next section, I propose a new version of Calibrationism and argue that it can avoid the conflict.

6 Evidence-Discounting Calibrationism

In this section, I defend a new version of Calibrationism, which I call 'Evidence-Discounting Calibrationism.' I argue that it's in a better position than existing versions in addressing the ignoring evidence problem and that it avoids the conflict with conditionalization. In Section 6.1, I give a rough formulation of the view. Section 6.2 explains its advantages over Credence-Calibrationism. Sections 6.3 and 6.4 refine the view. Section 6.5 argues that it avoids the conflict with conditionalization and that it better handles the problem of ignoring evidence than existing versions of Calibrationism. Section 6.6 explains why we should prefer Evidence-Discounting Calibrationism to a recent version of Calibrationism that invokes imprecise credence.

6.1 Evidence-Discounting Calibrationism: A Rough Formulation

Up till now, I've been using 'Calibrationism' to stand for 'Credence-Calibrationism.' Now I will use the two terms separately. Calibrationism says that one's credence in a proposition p should cohere with one's expected reliability with regard to whether p, where the expected reliability is arrived at independently of one's first-order reasoning. This thesis is not very clear since the notion of 'coherence' is not very clear. As I have mentioned in Section 3.1, Credence-Calibrationism is a more precise thesis. It says

(i) Bridge

One's credence in a proposition p should match one's expected reliability with regard to p.

(ii) Independence

One's expected reliability with regard to p should be arrived at independently of one's first-order reasoning.

So, according to Credence-Calibrationism, to say that our first-order attitudes should cohere with higher-order ones is to say that the two should exactly match.

In what follows, I propose a new version of Calibrationism by proposing a new way of cashing out the coherence relation between levels of attitudes. I claim that the thing we should calibrate is not our credence, but *the degree to which we rely on our first-order evidence* in forming credence. I call it Evidence-Discounting Calibrationism and give a rough formulation of the view here. I will refine the view later.

Evidence-Discounting Calibrationism (First Pass)

The degree to which one relies on one's first-order evidence should cohere with one's expected reliability.

Here, the term 'coherence' means some kind of nondecreasing function: as the expected reliability becomes greater, the degree to which one relies on one's first-order evidence doesn't decrease. I will clarify what this nondecreasing function should be in later sections, after I clarify the notion 'the degree to which one relies on one's first-order evidence.'

In the next section, I will explain why a Calibrationist should think that the thing we should calibrate to expected reliability about H is not credence in H but the degree to which we rely on our first-order evidence in forming credence in H.

When you gain evidence E, the degree to which you rely on E in your new credence in a proposition H can be seen as a matter of credence aggregation. Consider two imaginary counterparts of yours. One counterpart completely relies on E: she conditionalizes her prior credence in H on E. The other counterpart completely ignores E: she just retains her prior credence in H. (The two glosses of 'completely relying on E' and 'completely ignoring E' are only rough ones; more precise glosses will be provided later.) Then the degree to which you rely on E in your new credence in H is reflected in how you aggregate the two counterparts' credences. The closer your new credence is to the first counterpart's, the greater the degree to which you rely on E. So, suppose that you aggregate the two counterparts' credences in a linear way; that is, there is some value x in [0, 1] such that, when you gain evidence E, your new credence in H relates to your old credence in this way:

$$C_1(H) = xC_0(H/E) + (1 - x)C_0(H)$$

where C_1 is your new credence function, and C_0 is the credence function you and your counterparts hold before gaining E.[25] Then we can take x to be the degree to which you rely on E. The closer x is to 1, the greater the degree to which you rely on E in your credence in H.[26]

A clarification on the talk of the degree of relying on E is in order. 'The degree to which one relies on E' should be understood as a relational property – it's the degree of 'relying on E *as opposed to* relying on the evidence one would have if E is removed from one's total evidence.' My thought in the previous paragraph is that fully relying on the first-order evidence E means adopting $C_0(H/E)$, and fully relying on the evidence without E means adopting $C_0(H)$, so that if one's credence is a weighted average between the two, that weight can represent the degree to which 'one relies on E as opposed to the evidence without E.' So, strictly speaking, instead of saying 'degree of relying on E,' I should say 'degree of relying on E as opposed to evidence without E.' But I will stick with the shorter phrase 'degree of relying on E' for simplicity.

6.2 Why Evidence-Discounting Calibrationism Is Better Than Credence-Calibrationism

To see why Evidence-Discounting Calibrationism is better than Credence-Calibrationism, consider this scenario. Suppose you know that Adam is an expert about the weather, and he tells you that it's raining tomorrow. As you are about to assign a high credence in tomorrow's raining, you are told that Adam has recently suffered brain damage that causes him to make weather predictions entirely randomly: it's as if he flips a coin to decide whether to predict raining or predict not-raining. So, you know that the chance that he will give a correct prediction is only 50 percent. Given this information, should you set your credence in 'it's raining tomorrow' to 0.5?

---

[25] I assume linear aggregation merely for the sake of simplicity. I don't mean to suggest that linear aggregation is necessarily the correct method of aggregating credences. If it turns out that some other method of aggregation is correct, we will revise accordingly our method of reading 'the degree to which you rely on E' from the relationship between C_1 and C_0.

[26] What if there is no such value x in [0, 1] that satisfies the above equation; that is, any value x that satisfies this equation is either greater than 1 or smaller than 0? In this case, we can claim that, if x is greater than 1, then you have completely relied on E (i.e., the degree to which you rely on E is 100 percent); if x is smaller than 0, then you have completely ignored E (i.e., the degree to which you rely on E is 0 percent).

The answer is clearly negative. The information that Adam makes predictions entirely randomly only implies that *you can entirely ignore his prediction* in forming your credence about the weather. Since there is entirely no correlation between his prediction and the truth, you should just treat his prediction as completely irrelevant. And treating his prediction as completely irrelevant *doesn't* imply that you should be 0.5 confident in the proposition that he predicts; it only means that you *should not rely on* his prediction in forming your credence. That is, whatever credence you had before knowing his prediction, you should keep that credence.[27]

Now, consider a variant of this case. Adam doesn't suffer brain damage; he is as reliable as usual. However, this time, Adam doesn't directly tell you what his prediction is; instead, he writes his prediction down on a piece of paper. But due to his poor handwriting, you are not confident in what he has written. Suppose you can correctly figure out what he writes only 50 percent of the time; that is, it's as if you can only randomly guess whether he writes 'it's raining' or 'it's not raining.' The lesson we draw from the previous case carries over: this information doesn't imply that you should be 0.5 confident in the proposition that you guess is what Adam writes; it at best means that you shouldn't rely on Adam's writing in forming your credence, that is, you should treat his writing as completely irrelevant.

Now, tweak the case further: imagine that Adam is not a person; rather, it's your first-order evidence; you can correctly 'read' what your first-order evidence says only 50 percent of the times. The lesson drawn from this case should still apply: your expected reliability in assessing your first-order evidence *has no direct connection* with your credence; rather, it's only directly connected to *the degree to which you should rely on the evidence.* If you can only read your evidence in a way that has absolutely no correlation with what the evidence actually says, you should not rely on that evidence in forming credence; this only means that, in the equation

$$C_1(H) = xC_0(H/E) + (1 - x)C_0(H)$$

x should be set to 0. That is, it only tells you that $C_1(H)$ should be equal to $C_0(H)$ but doesn't tell you what specific value $C_1(H)$ should be.

In the previous paragraph, the relevant unreliability is unreliability in assessing your first-order evidence. As I explained in Section 1.1, this type of unreliability is a common reason – although not the only reason – why one is unreliable in

---

[27] From a Bayesian perspective, it's as if what you should update on is not what Adam says – namely, 'it's raining tomorrow' – but 'Adam predicts it's raining tomorrow.' If Adam's reliability is only 50 percent, then conditionalizing on the latter leads to a posterior credence in raining that's the same as the prior credence.

forming true judgments on the basis of one's first-order evidence. We have argued that what this unreliability directly implies is that you should not rely on your first-order evidence. What if you are unreliable in forming true judgments for other reasons? For instance, what if you have cognitive deficiencies in collecting evidence, so that the evidence you actually possess is not 'representative' enough? Or, what if your evidence just happens not to support what it usually supports due to some conditions that undercut the evidential connection?

The answer is clear: you should also not fully rely on your first-order evidence, since these factors indicate that there is something wrong with the evidence itself, so that fully relying on them is unlikely to lead you to truths. And assuming that we can meaningfully talk about the degree of which your evidence is unrepresentative and the degree to which the evidential support relation is undercut, it's meaningful and plausible to claim that these degrees should also affect the degree to which you rely on the evidence.

So, the lesson is this: when your HOE says that you are unreliable in forming true judgments on the basis of your first-order evidence, then, no matter for what reason you are unreliable (no matter whether the fault lies in you or lies in the first-order evidence itself), what the HOE directly requires is that you should not fully rely on the first-order evidence; it doesn't directly imply what credence is rational. This is the reason why Calibrationists should prefer Evidence-Discounting Calibrationism over Credence-Calibrationism.

6.3 Refining Evidence-Discounting Calibrationism: Second Pass

Before I explain the other virtues of Evidence-Discounting Calibrationism, I should make it more precise. The formulation of the view in Section 6.1 says that 'the degree to which one relies on one's first-order evidence should *cohere with* one's expected reliability.' And I've said that the term 'coherence' means some kind of nondecreasing function: as the expected reliability becomes greater, the degree to which one relies on one's first-order evidence doesn't decrease. Now, what exactly is the nondecreasing function?

First, the nondecreasing function cannot be simple identity. In Section 6.2, we discussed a case in which your expected reliability is 50 percent because you evaluate evidence in a way as if you're coin-flipping (i.e., if heads up you take E to support H; otherwise you take E to support not-H), but we've said that, in this case, the degree to which you should rely on E is 0 percent, not 50 percent. You should completely ignore the evidence if you can only randomly guess what it says, just like in the first weather forecast case, you should completely ignore Adam's prediction if you know that he made the prediction randomly.

Second, we can derive the correct nondecreasing function in the following way. Let's first make the following reasonable symmetry assumption: your reliability is not affected by the truth value of the proposition in question. That is, you are no more (and no less) likely to form a correct judgment about the proposition when it is true than when it is false. This assumption ensures that a 50 percent reliability implies perfect uncorrelation; that is, from C(H and I judge H) + C(not-H and I judge not-H) = 0.5, we have C(I judge H/H) = C(I judge H/not-H).[28] And intuitively, in perfect uncorrelation (such as random guessing), you should completely ignore evidence.

Then, note that, when your reliability degree is between 50 percent and 100 percent, we can view the way you form judgments as a probability-mixture of two extreme cases of correlation – a case of perfect correlation and a case of perfect uncorrelation. This is because your expected reliability can be viewed as a probability-mixture of 100 percent reliability degree and 50 percent reliability degree. That is, if your expected reliability is r (where r is between 100 and 50 percent), there is some value x in [0, 1] such that

$$r = x100\% + (1 - x)50\% \tag{1}$$

This means that, when your expected reliability is r, it's as if you are x confident that you form judgment in a way that's perfectly correlated with the truth, and (1-x) confident that you form judgment in a way that's perfectly uncorrelated with the truth (recall that, given our symmetry assumption, 50 percent expected reliability implies perfect uncorrelation). This in turn means that you are x confident that you should rely on evidence to the degree of 100 percent and (1-x) confident that you should rely on evidence to the degree of 0 percent. Therefore, the rational degree to which you should rely on evidence can be taken as a weighted average between the two extreme values, and it seems natural to take the weight to be x. So, when your expected reliability is r, you should rely on evidence to degree $x \cdot 100\% + (1-x) \cdot 0\%$, which is simply x. And since Equation (1) tells us that x = 2(r − 0.5), we have this result:

---

[28] Proof: C(I form a correct judgment about whether H) = C(I judge H and H) + C(I judge not-H and not-H) = C(I judge H /H)&C(H) + C(I judge not-H/not-H)&C(not-H). Given the symmetry assumption, we have C(I judge H/H) = C(I judge not-H/not-H). So, if C(I form a correct judgment about whether H) = 0.5, we have C(I judge H/H) = C(I judge not-H/not-H) = 0.5. But since C(I judge not-H/not-H) + C(I judge H/not-H) = 1, we have C(I judge H/not-H) = 0.5; therefore, we have C(I judge H/H) = C(I judge H/not-H).

You might think that, for this proof to go through, we need an additional assumption: I'm certain that I will make a judgment about H. But this assumption is not necessary. If there is a positive probability that I don't make a judgment, then 'my expected reliability is 0.5' should not be taken to imply C(I form a correct judgment about H) = 0.5 but rather imply the conditional credence C(I form a correct judgment about H/ I make a judgment about H) = 0.5. And the proof still goes through if we replace all terms in it with similar conditional versions.

If your expected reliability degree is r, where r is between 100 percent and 50 percent, you should rely on your evidence to degree 2(r-0.5).

What about the case where you expect yourself to be *anti-reliable*, when the expected reliability is between 0 percent and 50 percent? The answer is clear: since your degree of reliance on E should be 0 percent when your expected reliability is exactly 50 percent, and since your degree of reliance on E should be a nondecreasing function of your expected reliability, it follows that your degree of reliance on E should also be 0 percent when your expected reliability is below 50 percent. So,

If your expected reliability degree is r, where r is between 0 percent and 50 percent, you should rely on your evidence to degree 0 percent.

These results give us the following refined formulation of Evidential-Discounting Calibrationism:

Evidence-Discounting Calibrationism (Second Pass)

Let w refer to the degree to which one should rely on one's first-order evidence, and let r refer to one's expected reliability. Then w should be a nondecreasing function of r in this way:

$$w = 2(r-0.5), \text{ if } r > 0.5;$$
$$w = 0, \text{if } r \leq 0.5.$$

Again, what expected reliability directly influences is the degree to which one should rely on one's first-order evidence E in forming one's credence in H. Expected reliability influences one's credence in H only indirectly: given a degree of reliance w, one's credence in H should be an aggregate of $C_0(H/E)$ and $C_0(H)$, where C_0 is a rational initial prior, and the weight of the aggregation is w. If we assume linear aggregation, then one's credence in H should satisfy:

$$C_1(H) = wC_0(H/E) + (1 - w)C_0(H) \tag{2}$$

For instance, if your expected reliability is 0.7, then you should rely on your first-order evidence to degree 0.4; this means that your credence in H should be $0.4C_0(H/E) + 0.6C_0(H)$.

6.4 Evidence-Discounting Calibrationism: Third Pass

Equation (2) is still not quite the formulation that I want to ultimately defend, since it has the following implausible implication: when your expected reliability r is between 0 percent and 50 percent, the exact value of r makes no difference to what credence one should have in H, since one should just adopt $C_0(H)$ for any r that is between 0 percent and 50 percent. But it's implausible that the degree to which one is *anti-reliable* makes no difference to which credence is rational. Presumably, if one initially judges H, one's credence in H should gradually decrease as one's expected reliability gradually decreases from 50 percent to 0 percent.[29]

Here is a more serious worry: Suppose $C_0(H) = 0.6$ and $C_0(H/E) = 0.8$. That is, E confirms H relative to C_0. Now suppose that one receives a body of HOE that suggests that one is *anti-reliable* in judging the truth of H on the basis of E. Given this, the Calibrationist will presumably want to say that this HOE should lead one to reduce one's credence in H to a point below 0.6. To see this, let's suppose that the HOE says that one is perfectly anti-reliable; that is, one's reliability is 0 percent. Then, one's HOE gives one conclusive evidence that one's judgment that H is false, which means that one's credence in H should become 0. However, no weighted average of 0.6 and 0.8 will result in a credence lower than 0.6. Thus, it looks like Evidence-Discounting Calibrationism cannot give the right verdict in this kind of case.

So, Equation (2) is not quite right. Here is a plausible way of tweaking it to avoid these problems. Throughout Sections 6.2 and 6.3, I've been relying on the following two glosses of 'fully ignoring E' (or 'giving E no weight') and 'fully relying on E' (or 'giving E full weight'): to say that one gives E no weight is to say that one just retains the prior credence $C_0(H)$, and to say that one gives E full weight is to say that one conditionalizes the prior credence in H on E; that is, to have credence $C_0(H/E)$.

But these two glosses are not quite right. We have stipulated that E is all the first-order evidence bearing on H *before* one gains HOE; however, the HOE (combined with information of what one's judgment is) might give one *new* first-order evidence bearing on H. In particular, if we suppose that one is certain that one judges H on the basis of E, then gaining HOE that one is anti-reliable in reaching a true judgment about H on the basis of E gives one *new first-order evidence* against H. For instance, if the HOE says that one's reliability degree is 0, it gives one conclusive first-order evidence against H. And in this case, although the HOE requires one to give no weight to E, it certainly shouldn't require one to retain one's prior credence. This is because the HOE of one's unreliability is about one's unreliability in forming true judgments on the basis of one's *old* first-order evidence E; therefore, the HOE should require one to bracket only that old

---

[29] I'm grateful to an anonymous reviewer for raising this worry and the worry discussed in the following paragraph.

first-order evidence, and the new first-order evidence provided by one's HOE should not be ignored.

This observation motivates the following revision of Equation (2): when the HOE says that one's reliability is below 50 percent and thus requires one to give no weight to E, one's new credence should not be $C_0(H)$ but be $C_0(H/I$ judge H & HOE), and this value can be calculated in the following way:

$$C_1(H) = C_0(H/I \text{ judge } H \text{ \& HOE})$$
$$= C_0(I \text{ judge } H/H \text{ \& HOE})C_0(H/HOE)/C_0(I \text{ judge } H/H \text{ \& HOE})$$
$$C_0(H/HOE) + C_0(I \text{ judge } H/\text{not-}H \text{ \& HOE})C_0(\text{not-}H/HOE)$$

Since HOE doesn't by itself bear on H, $C_0(H/HOE)$ can be simplified as $C_0(H)$ and $C_0(\text{not-}H/HOE)$ can be simplified as $C_0(\text{not-}H)$. So, if the HOE says that one's reliability degree is r, where $r \leq 0.5$, we have

$$C_1(H) = C_0(H/I \text{ judge } H \text{ \& HOE}) = rC_0(H)/rC_0(H) + (1-r)(1-C_0(H))$$

This value is identical to $C_0(H)$ if $r = 0.5$, but smaller than $C_0(H)$ if $r < 0.5$, So, it accords with the intuition that when the HOE says that one's judgment is the result of a random process, one should just retain one's prior credence; it also implies that one should adopt a credence smaller than $C_0(H)$ if one initially judges H on the basis of E and then receives HOE that one is anti-reliable.

Similarly, in the case in which one should give E full weight, one's new credence in H should not simply be $C_0(H/E)$; rather, it should be $C_0(H/E$ & I judge H & HOE), and a similar calculation shows that this value could be simplified as $rC_0(H/E)/rC_0(H/E) + (1-r)(1-C_0(H/E))$.

With these revisions, the equation

$$C_1(H) = wC_0(H/E) + (1-w)C_0(H) \tag{2}$$

should be revised into

$$C_1(H) = wC(H/E) + (1-w)C(H) \tag{3}$$

where C(H) is $C_0(H)$ conditionalized on HOE and the information 'I judge H,' which is $rC_0(H)/rC_0(H) + (1-r)(1-C_0(H))$, and C(H/E) is $C_0(H/E)$ conditionalized on HOE and the information 'I judge H,' which is $rC_0(H/E)/rC_0(H/E) + (1-r)(1-C_0(H/E))$.

Now, we can reformulate Evidence-Discounting Calibrationism as follows:

Evidence-Discounting Calibrationism (Third Pass)

Let w refer to the degree to which one should rely on one's first-order evidence, and let r refer to one's expected reliability. Then w should be a nondecreasing function of r in this way:

$$w = 2(r - 0.5), \text{ if } r > 0.5;$$
$$w = 0, \text{ if } r \leq 0.5.$$

And this degree of reliance w helps determine one's new credence when gaining HOE according to Equation (3).

Let's consider a specific case to see how this proposal works. Suppose that $C_0(H)$, one's initial credence in H before gaining any evidence, is 0.6; one then gains evidence E, which supports H, and $C_0(H/E) = 0.8$; so, one's credence increases to 0.8; then one gains HOE saying that one's reliability degree is 0.2. The impact of this reliability information is two-fold: it helps determine how confident one should be if one gives no weight to E as well as how confident one should be if one gives full weight to E; besides, it also determines how much weight one should give to E. In this case, the giving-no-weight-to E credence (which is C(H) in Equation (3)) should be 0.27, the giving-full-weight-to-E credence (which is C(H/E) in Equation (3)) should be 0.5, and the weight given to E (which is w in Equation (3)) should be 0. So, if Equation (3) is correct, one's new credence in H should be 0.27. If we change the case into one where one's HOE says that one's reliability degree is 0.7, then the giving-no-weight-to E credence should be 0.78, the giving-full-weight-to-E credence should be 0.9, and the weight given to E should be 0.4, which means that one's new credence in H should be 0.83.

6.5 Virtues of Evidence-Discounting Calibrationism

In this section, I argue that Evidence-Discounting Calibrationism has many virtues compared to existing versions of Calibrationism. In particular, it avoids the conflict with conditionalization, and it's in a better position than all existing versions in dealing with the problem of ignoring evidence.

6.5.1 The Conflict with Conditionalization

First, White's argument that Credence-Calibrationism conflicts with conditionalization doesn't apply to Evidence-Discounting Calibrationism. The conflict arises because Credence-Calibrationism requires one's credence in H to be identical with one's expected reliability. But according to Evidence-Discounting Calibrationism, there is no direct relation between the two. One's expected reliability directly influences how much one should rely on one's first-order evidence, or how much weight one should give to one's evidence. But as Equation (3) shows, how this should in turn influence one's credence in H depends on what credence one should have when one gives the first-order evidence full weight and what credence one should have when one gives the evidence no weight.

For a similar reason, Evidence-Discounting Calibrationism doesn't commit the base-rate fallacy. Unlike Credence-Calibrationism, which says that one's credence is dictated by expected reliability, Evidence-Discounting Calibrationism allows the influence of priors. Equation (3) tells us that one's priors (including both the priors one has before one acquires HOE and also the priors one has before one even acquires E) have an impact on one's rational credence in H.

6.5.2 The Problem of Ignoring Evidence

Evidence-Discounting Calibrationism is in a better position than other versions of Calibrationism in handling the problem of ignoring evidence. In Section 4.3, we've seen that some Credence-Calibrationists regard ignoring evidence as exactly the right thing to do when one has HOE and they've offered an accuracy-argument for the claim. As I've mentioned there, a problem with their argument is that it seems to prove too much, because it tells us to ignore evidence not only when our expected reliability is low, but also when it's high, and this is counterintuitive. It seems that, when the risk of forming false judgments on the basis of evidence is small, the risk is worth taking for the potential benefit brought by using a larger body of evidence.

It's not just Credence-Calibrationists that require ignoring evidence regardless of how high one's expected reliability is. Horowitz and Sliva's (2015) Evidential Calibrationism faces the same problem. As we've seen in Section 4.2.2, Evidential Calibrationism accommodates the direction of evidence, but it still ignores evidential strength no matter how high one's expected reliability is, because it requires calibrating credence in the proposition supported by evidence to expected reliability, no matter what that expected reliability degree is.

Besides Credence-Calibrationism and Evidential Calibrationism, there is another version of Calibrationism in the literature that also requires ignoring evidence no matter how high one's expected reliability is. It's inspired by the thought that 'judgment screens off evidence when we have HOE' (see Weatherson, n.d.). Basically, it says that the correct way of responding to HOE is to conditionalize the credence you held before gaining E, not on information E, but on information about what you judge on the basis of E. That is, if you judge H on the basis of E, then

$C_1(H) = Cr(H/I \text{ judge } H)$

where Cr is a credence function without information E but informed by HOE, such that $Cr(I \text{ judge } H/H) = Cr(I \text{ judge not-}H/\text{not-}H) = $ the expected reliability degree specified by the HOE.

We can call this version Updating-on-Judgment Calibrationism. This version of Calibrationism also ignores evidence in an implausible way. Why think that no matter what your expected reliability degree is, you should always update only on information about what you judge on the basis of E but not on the information E itself? Again, the problem is this: perhaps you should ignore E when your expected reliability in forming true judgments on the basis of E is low, but why ignore E when your expected reliability is high?

Unlike all the three versions of Calibrationism discussed, Evidence-Discounting Calibrationism doesn't claim that we should ignore evidence no matter what our expected reliability degree is. It claims that we should ignore evidence when the expected reliability is at best 50 percent, but when expected reliability is higher than 50 percent, we should *discount* evidence rather than *ignoring* it, and the rate of discount is determined by the expected reliability degree. In particular, evidential strength *does* matter to what credence we should have: Equation (3), which says that $C_1(H) = wC(H/E) + (1-w)C(H)$, tells us that the degree to which E supports H can influence the rational credence in H when our total evidence is E&HOE.

Of course, there is still the residual worry that Evidence-Discounting Calibrationism requires ignoring evidence when expected reliability is at best 50 percent. But I submit that this shouldn't be regarded as a problem for Evidence-Discounting Calibrationism or a problem for Calibrationism in general; *rather, it reveals deep disagreement between Calibrationism and the Steadfastness on the normativity of evidence*. The Steadfasters are committed to a fundamentalist view about the normativity of evidence. According to this view, evidence has intrinsic normative power. Evidence cannot be ignored, unless you have reason to doubt its credential – say, when you have reason to doubt that it's misleading or that it's gained in a biased way. But when your expected reliability is low, you should first suspect that it's because you have cognitive deficiency in assessing (first-order) evidence – after all, in typical HOE cases, such a kind of deficiency is the most common reason why one is unlikely to reach true judgments on the basis of one's first-order evidence. And evidence of cognitive deficiency in assessing evidence is not reason to doubt the quality or the credential of the evidence. When you have low expected reliability in assessing the evidence, you should still think that the evidence is good evidence and it's just that you are unable to properly use it. But inability to properly use evidence, according to the Steadfaster, is not a reason not to use it (although it might be an excuse). For these fundamentalists, the normative significance of evidence for an agent doesn't depend on the agent's abilities in assessing evidence.

By contrast, Calibrationists think that inability to properly use evidence, or evidence of such inability, is a reason not to use the evidence. For the Calibrationist, evidence is merely a tool we use for gaining truths. So, when you are told that you are not very capable in using that tool for the purpose of gaining truths, you should not use the tool, and this is so even if you have no reason to doubt that the tool itself is defective. Again, the knife analogy I've mentioned in Section 2.1 is helpful: when you are told that you are not very capable in properly using the knife for the purpose of cutting (due to some disease), you should not use it for cutting, and this is so even if you have no reason to doubt that the knife itself is defective.

Aside from appealing to analogy, the Calibrationist can also appeal to a broadly responsibilist view on the normativity of evidence, in order to explain why inability or evidence of inability to properly use evidence affects the normative power of evidence. According to this view, evidence doesn't have intrinsic normative power. When you have independent reason to think that you are incapable of properly using your evidence for the purpose of gaining truths, it's intellectually irresponsible to use your evidence.[30] And such a kind of irresponsibility can often be revealed by the criticizability of the action that one is allowed to take on the Steadfastness view: suppose that a doctor refuses to withdraw his diagnosis when he gains evidence that he is likely to misevaluate his evidence due to sleep deprivation, and suppose that based on his diagnosis, he prescribes certain drugs to the patient. It's intuitive to think that the doctor's action is criticizable, and such kind of criticizability in action shows that the doctor's belief about his diagnosis is intellectually irresponsible (Steel, 2019).

What about Kelly's worry that ignoring evidence makes rationality come by too easily? The Evidence-Discounting Calibrationist will just admit that, when your expected reliability is low, it's indeed easy to be rational, because what your first-order evidence E supports doesn't matter. But when your expected reliability is high, what E supports does matter: if your credence $C(H/E)$ is not a rational one, then obeying Evidence-Discounting Calibrationism by following Equation (3) (that is, by setting your credence in H to $wC(H/E) + (1 - w)C(H)$) won't necessarily give you a rational

---

[30] For a detailed explanation appealing to intellectual responsibility, see Ye (2020).

credence in H. So, here, the familiar saying 'With great power comes great responsibility' applies: in order to reach a rational credence in H, a person whose expected reliability is high has to do more work than a person whose expected reliability is low.

Last, there is the worry that ignoring evidence conflicts with the principle of not ignoring free evidence, a principle that's justified by Good's theorem. According to the theorem, free evidence is always valuable: acting after we gain the free evidence has greater expected utility than acting without it.

Here is my response. Good's proof assumes that you are certain that you will obey the rule of conditionalization if you get the new evidence. That is, it assumes that, if you perform the inquiry of finding out which evidence in the partition {E, not-E} you will get, you will update to $C_0(/E)$ if you learn E, and you will update to $C_0(/\text{not-E})$ if you learn not-E. But if you now have HOE that tells you that your expected reliability in forming true judgments on the basis of the evidence is low, you should suspect that you are unlikely to correctly evaluate your new evidence, which means that this assumption that you will succeed in following the rule of conditionalization doesn't obtain. If you think that you are very likely to misevaluate your new evidence, then you should think that, *even if* you learn E, it's very likely that you will not update your credence to $C_0(/E)$.

For instance, let p be a proposition that's entailed by E but the entailment is not obvious, or at least, it's not obvious to you when you are cognitively impaired. Suppose you know that you will be cognitively impaired when you gain E. Then although $C_0(p/E) = 1$ (assuming that your cognitive abilities are normal now), you should think it likely that you will not see the connection between E and p if you gain E at the next moment, and thus it's likely that your new credence in p will not be 1 when you learn E.

6.6 Evidence-Discounting Calibrationism versus Imprecise Calibrationism

Recently, Henderson (in press) has proposed a new version of Calibrationism by appealing to imprecise credence. She argues that we should represent a doxastic attitude as having two dimensions: a substantive dimension that represents one's level of uncertainty, and a conviction dimension that represents one's level of confidence in the rationality of one's uncertainty. She also suggests that this two-dimensional framework can be cashed out in terms of imprecise credence; in particular, the level of conviction can be cashed out in terms of the level of precision in an imprecise credence. (For instance, a credal state [0, 1] has the same level of uncertainty as the credal state {0.5}, but it has a lower level of conviction since it's more imprecise.)

Based on this imprecise credence framework, Henderson has defended a new version of Calibrationism that can be called 'Imprecise Calibrationism.' It says that what expected reliability mainly affects is not how high your credence is, but how *precise* your credence is. The lower your expected reliability is, the more imprecise your credence should be. More specifically, when the rational credence in H given your first-order evidence E alone is $C_0(H/E)$, and when you gain HOE implying that your expected reliability is r, your new credence in H should be:

$$C_1(H) = rC_0(H/E) + (1 - r)(0, 1) \text{ (IP)}$$

The term on the right side of equation IP refers to a credence interval (a, b), where $b = rC_0(H/E) + (1 - r)1$, and $a = rC_0(H/E) + (1 - r)0$. This equation implies that, given a fixed body of first-order evidence, the lower your expected reliability is, the more weight should be given to the extreme imprecise credence (0, 1), and thus the more imprecise your credence should be. So, Imprecise Calibrationism basically says that what we should calibrate to expected reliability is the degree of precision in our credence.

In form, Imprecise Calibrationism is quite similar to Evidence-Discounting Calibrationism, which, as we recall, says $C_1(H) = wC(H/E) + (1 - w)C(H)$, where $w = 2(r - 0.5)$ if $r > 0.5$, and $w = 0$ otherwise. But Evidence-Discounting Calibrationism is better than Imprecise Calibrationism in two respects.

First, Imprecise Calibrationism gives implausible recommendations in those cases where one gains *positive* kind of HOE, namely, the kind of HOE which says that one's reliability is high. For it says that one will lose conviction even if one gains HOE which says that one is highly (although not perfectly) reliable. Consider this case: suppose that one starts out with a precise 0.8 credence in H and then gains HOE that says that one is 99.99 percent reliable. Imprecise Calibrationism implies that one's new credence should be an interval, which is more imprecise than one's initial credence. Since Henderson thinks that the level of precision represents the level of conviction in the rationality of one's uncertainty, she will have to say that one should lose conviction in this case; that is, one should be less confident that one's level of uncertainty is rational. But this is counterintuitive. Presumably, the HOE that says that one is extremely reliable should come as good news.

Second, Imprecise Calibrationism is less well motivated than Evidence-Discounting Calibrationism. Even if we accept Henderson's basic idea that gaining HOE reduces the precision of one's credence, we are still owed an explanation why the reduction should be cashed out in the form of equation (IP) rather than in some other form. In particular, why should one's new credence be a weighted average of the old credence and *the extreme imprecise credence (0, 1)?*

Of course, Henderson can respond by saying that (IP) can be motivated by the same thought that I have used to motivate Evidence-Discounting Calibrationism; that is, one's new credence should be a weighted average of the old credence and *the extreme imprecise credence*, because it should be a weighted average of a credence that gives one's original evidence full weight and a credence that *gives one's original evidence no weight*, and giving one's original evidence no weight means adopting the absolute prior credence $C_0(H)$, a credence that one should have when one has no evidence; then Henderson can continue the story by saying that the absolute prior credence $C_0(H)$ should just be the extreme imprecise credence (0, 1).

Although this explanation can motivate (IP), it will commit the Imprecise Calibrationist to the controversial position that, for any proposition H, one's absolute prior credence $C_0(H)$ should be the extreme imprecise credence (0, 1). By contrast, Evidence-Discounting Calibrationism incurs no such commitment. Evidence-Discounting Calibrationism is simply silent on what the absolute prior $C_0(H)$ should be, and this is exactly the right thing to do: Calibrationists need not commit to a general theory about what one's credence in a proposition should be when one has no evidence. Perhaps the imprecise credence (0, 1) is warranted, or perhaps a sharp 0.5 credence is called for in some circumstance, or perhaps a permissivist stance applies such that any sharp credence within the interval (0, 1) is rational.

To sum up, in this section, I have proposed and defended Evidence-Discounting Calibrationism. The core idea of this view is that the thing we should calibrate to expected reliability is not our credence in the first-order proposition H, but the degree to which we should rely on our first-order evidence in forming credence in H. This calibration will influence our credence in H, because our credence in H should be an aggregate of the credence we would have if we entirely relied on the evidence and the credence we would have if we entirely ignored the evidence, where the aggregation is weighted by the degree to which we should rely on the evidence. I have argued that Evidence-Discounting Calibrationism has several virtues that existing versions of Calibrationism don't have, including avoiding the conflict with conditionalization and handling the problem of ignoring evidence.

7 Conclusion

Higher-order evidence is evidence not about the world but evidence of our own fallibility, such as evidence about whether our belief is formed in a rational or reliable way. The debate on higher-order evidence is about whether, and how exactly, higher-order evidence should influence our first-order belief. This Element is devoted to defending the view that higher-order evidence has a significant impact on our first-order belief through affecting the degree to which we should rely on first-order evidence. I've called this view 'Evidence-Discounting Calibrationism.' Unlike the traditional version of Calibrationism, which says that higher-order evidence directly dictates our first-order credence, Evidence-Discounting Calibrationism says that higher-order evidence only directly dictates the degree to which we rely on first-order evidence. I have argued that this change in the answer to the question 'what exactly is it the thing that we should calibrate to expected reliability' has many virtues compared to existing versions of Calibrationism.

Here is a summary of earlier sections. Section 1 clarifies the debate on higher-order evidence and explains why the debate is important. Section 2 explains the three major positions in the debate, one of which is Calibrationism. Section 3 discusses the most popular version of Calibrationism, called 'Credence-Calibrationism,' and argues that existing motivations for Credence-Calibrationism are unsuccessful. Section 4 and Section 5 discuss the two most important challenges that Credence-Calibrationism faces: the problem of ignoring evidence and the conflict with conditionalization; criticisms of existing answers to these challenges are offered. Section 6 defends Evidence-Discounting Calibrationism and argues that it can handle the two problems satisfactorily.

There are many issues surrounding HOE and Calibrationism that this Element doesn't have the space to address, including but not limited to (a) the self-defeating objection against Conciliationism (Matheson, 2015; Pittard, 2015), (b) whether the independence principle leads to skepticism (Christensen, 2011, pp. 15–18; Vavova, 2018), (c) how to formulate a plausible level-bridging principle about the connection between first-order credence and expected rational credence (rather than expected reliability; see Dorst [2020], Elga [2013], and Lasonen-Aarnio [2015]), (d) whether evidence of evidence is evidence (Tal & Comesana, 2017; Williamson, 2019), and so on. But I hope that this Element, though limited in scope, has presented some reason to think that the broad debate on higher-order evidence is both interesting and important for thinking about a range of other important debates in epistemology.

References

Beddor, B. (2015). Process reliabilism's troubles with defeat. *Philosophical Quarterly*, *65*(259), 145–59.

Bradley, D. (2020a). Self-locating belief and updating on learning. *Mind*, *129*(514), 579–84.

Bradley, D. (2020b). Bayesianism and self-doubt. *Synthese*, *199*(1–2), 2225–43.

Bykvist, K. (2017). Moral ignorance. *Philosophy Compass*, *12*(3), e12408.

Christensen, D. (2007). Does Murphy's law apply in epistemology? Self-doubt and rational ideals. *Oxford Studies in Epistemology*, *2*, 3–31.

Christensen, D. (2009). Disagreement as evidence: The epistemology of controversy. *Philosophy Compass*, *4*(5), 756–67.

Christensen, D. (2010). Higher-order evidence. *Philosophy and Phenomenological Research*, *81*(1), 185–215.

Christensen, D. (2011). Disagreement, question-begging, and epistemic self-criticism. *Philosophers' Imprint*, *11*, 1–22.

Christensen, D. (2016a). Conciliation, uniqueness and rational toxicity. *Noûs*, *50*, 584–603.

Christensen, D. (2016b). Disagreement, drugs, etc.: From accuracy to akrasia. *Episteme*, *13*(4), 397–422.

Christensen, D. (2019). Formulating independence. In M. Skipper & A. Steglich-Petersen (eds.), *Higher-Order Evidence: New Essays*. Oxford: Oxford University Press, pp. 13–34.

DiPaolo, J. (2019). Second best epistemology: Fallibility and normativity. *Philosophical Studies*, *176*(8), 2043–66.

Dorst, K. (2019). Higher-order uncertainty. In M. Skipper & A. Steglich-Petersen (eds.), *Higher-Order Evidence: New Essays*. Oxford: Oxford University Press, pp. 35–61.

Dorst, K. (2020). Evidence: A guide for the uncertain. *Philosophy and Phenomenological Research*, *100*(3), 586–632.

Dorst, K. (in press). Higher-order evidence. In M. Lasonen-Aarnio & C. Littlejohn (eds.), *The Routledge Handbook for the Philosophy of Evidence*. Routledge.

Elga, A. (2007). Reflection and disagreement. *Noûs*, *41*, 478–502.

Elga, A. (2013). The puzzle of the unmarked clock and the new rational reflection principle. *Philosophical Studies*, *164*(1), 127–39.

Elga, A. (n.d.). Lucky to be rational. Unpublished manuscript.

Feldman, R. (2005). Respecting the evidence. *Philosophical Perspectives*, *19*, 95–119.

Fitelson, B. & Jehle, D. (2009). What is the 'Equal Weight View'? *Episteme*, *6*(3), 280–93.

Foley, R. (1990). Fumerton's puzzle. *Journal of Philosophical Research*, *15*, 109–13.

Frances, B. (2010). The reflective epistemic renegade. *Philosophy and Phenomenological Research*, *81*(2), 419–63.

Gallow, J. D. (2019). Diachronic Dutch books and evidential import, *Philosophy and Phenomenological* Research *99*(1), 49–80.

González de Prado, J. (2020). Dispossessing Defeat. *Philosophy and Phenomenological Research*, *101*(2), 323–40.

Good, I. J. (1967). On the principle of total evidence. *The British Journal for the Philosophy of Science*, *17*(4), 319–21.

Greaves, H. & Wallace, D. (2006). Justifying conditionalization: Conditionalization maximizes expected epistemic utility. *Mind*, 115(459), 607–32.

Greco, D. (2019). Fragmentation and higher-order evidence. In M. Skipper & A. Steglich-Petersen (eds.), *Higher-Order Evidence: New Essays*. Oxford: Oxford University Press, pp. 84–104.

Hazlett, A. (2012). Higher-order epistemic attitudes and intellectual humility. *Episteme*, *9*, 205–23.

Henderson, L. (in press). Higher-order evidence and losing one's conviction. *Noûs*.

Horowitz, S. (2014). Epistemic akrasia. *Noûs*, *48*, 718–44.

Horowitz, S. & Sliwa, P. (2015). Respecting all the evidence. *Philosophical Studies*, *172*, 2835–58.

Huemer, M. (2011). The puzzle of metacoherence. *Philosophy and Phenomenological Research*, *82*(1), 1–21.

Ichikawa, J. & Jarvis, B. (2013). *The Rules of Thought*. Oxford: Oxford University Press.

Isaacs, Y. (2021). The fallacy of calibrationism. *Philosophy and Phenomenological Research*, *102*(2), 247–60.

Joyce J. M. (1998). A nonpragmatic vindication of probabilism. *Philosophy of Science*, *65*(4), 575–603.

Kelly, T. (2010). Peer disagreement and higher order evidence. In A. I. Goldman & D. Whitcomb (eds.), *Social Epistemology: Essential Readings*. Oxford: Oxford University Press, pp. 183–217.

Kelly, T. (2014). Evidence can be permissive. In M. Steup, J. Turri, & E. Sosa (eds.), *Contemporary Debates in Epistemology* (2nd ed.). Chichester: Wiley-Blackwell, pp. 298–312.

Lackey, J. (2008). A justificationist view of disagreement's epistemic significance. In A. Millar, A. Haddock, & D. Pritchard (eds.), *Social Epistemology*. Oxford: Oxford University Press. pp. 145–54.

Lasonen-Aarnio, M. (2010). Unreasonable knowledge. *Philosophical Perspectives*, *24*(1), 1–21.

Lasonen-Aarnio, M. (2014). Higher-order evidence and the limits of defeat. *Philosophy and Phenomenological Research*, *88*(2), 314–45.

Lasonen-Aarnio, M. (2015). New rational reflection and internalism about rationality. *Oxford Studies in Epistemology*, *5*, 145–79.

Lasonen-Aarnio, M. (2020). Enkrasia or evidentialism? *Philosophical Studies*, *177*, 597–632.

Levi, I. (1980). *The Enterprise of Knowledge: An Essay on Knowledge, Credal Probability, and Chance*. Cambridge: The MIT Press.

Levinstein, B. A. (n.d.). Higher-order evidence as information loss. Unpublished manuscript.

Littlejohn, C. (2018). Stop making sense? *Philosophy and Phenomenological Research*, *96*(2), 257–72.

Loewer, B. & Laddaga, R. (1985). Destroying the consensus. *Synthese 62*(1), 79–95.

Lord, E. (2014). From independence to conciliationism: An obituary. *Australasian Journal of Philosophy*, *92*(2), 365–77.

Matheson, J. (2015). Are conciliatory views of disagreement self-defeating? *Social Epistemology*, *29*(2), 145–59.

Neta, R. (2018). Evidence, coherence and epistemic akrasia. *Episteme*, *15*(3), 313–28.

Pittard, J. (2015). Resolute conciliationism. *Philosophical Quarterly*, *65*(260), 442–63.

Pritchard, D. (2014). Truth as the fundamental epistemic good. In J. Matheson & R. Vitz (eds.), *The Ethics of Belief: Individual and Social*. Oxford: Oxford University Press, pp. 112–29.

Rasmussen, M. S., Steglich-Petersen, A., & Bjerring, J. C. (2018). A higher-order approach to disagreement. *Episteme*, *15*(1), 80–100.

Roush, S. (2009). Second guessing: A self-help manual, *Episteme 6*(3), 251–68.

Schoenfield, M. (2014). Permission to believe. *Noûs*, *48*, 193–218.

Schoenfield, M. (2015). A dilemma for calibrationism. *Philosophy and Phenomenological Research*, *91*(2), 425–55.

Schoenfield, M. (2018). An accuracy based approach to higher-order evidence. *Philosophy and Phenomenological Research*, *96*(3), 690–715.

Sepielli, A. (2014). What to do when you don't know what to do when you don't know what to do . . .. *Noûs*, *48*(3), 521–44.

Shogenji, T. (2007). A conundrum in Bayesian epistemology of disagreement. Unpublished manuscript.

Skipper, M. (2019). Higher-order evidence and the impossibility of self-misleading evidence. In M. Skipper & A. Steglich-Petersen (eds.), *Higher-Order Evidence: New Essays*. Oxford: Oxford University Press, pp. 189–208.

Skipper, M. (2021). Does rationality demand higher-order certainty? *Synthese*, *198*(12), 11561–85.

Skipper, M. (2022). Higher-order evidence and the normativity of logic. In S. Stapleford, K. McCain, & M. Steup (eds.), *Epistemic Dilemmas: New Arguments, New Angles*. New York: Routledge, pp. 21–37.

Skipper, M. & Bjerring, J. C. (2020). Bayesianism for non-ideal agents. *Erkenntnis*, *87*(1), 93–115.

Smithies, D. (2012). Moore's paradox and the accessibility of justification. *Philosophy and Phenomenological Research*, *85*(2), 273–300.

Smithies, D. (2015). Ideal rationality and logical omniscience. *Synthese*, *192*(9), 2769–93.

Staffel, J. (in press). Transitional attitudes and the unmooring view of higher-order evidence. *Noûs*. https://doi.org/10.1111/nous.12400.

Steel, R. (2018). Anticipating failure and avoiding it. *Philosophers' Imprint*, *18*, 1–28.

Steel, R. (2019). Against right reason. *Philosophy and Phenomenological Research*, *99*(2), 431–60.

Street, S. (2006). A Darwinian dilemma for realist theories of value. *Philosophical Studies*, *127*, 109–66.

Tal, E. (2021). Disagreement and easy bootstrapping. *Episteme*, *18*(1), 46–65.

Tal, E. & Comesaña, J. (2017). Is evidence of evidence evidence? *Noûs*, *55*(1), 96–112.

Titelbaum, M. (2015). Rationality's fixed point (or: In defense of right reason). In J. Hawthorne & T. Gendler (eds.), *Oxford Studies in Epistemology, 5*. Oxford: Oxford University Press, pp. 253–94.

van Wietmarschen, H. (2013). Peer disagreement, evidence, and well-groundedness. *Philosophical Review*, *122*(3), 395–425.

Vavova, K. (2018). Irrelevant influences. *Philosophy and Phenomenological Research*, *96*(1), 134–52.

Weatherson, B. (n.d.). Do judgments screen evidence? Unpublished manuscript.

White, R. (2005). Epistemic permissiveness. *Philosophical Perspectives*, *19*(1), 445–59.

White, R. (2009). On treating oneself and others as thermometers. *Episteme*, *6*, 233–50.

White, R. (2010). You just believe that because... *Philosophical Perspectives*, *24*, 573–615.

Whiting, D. (in press). Recent work on higher-order evidence. *Analysis*.

Williamson, T. (2000). *Knowledge and Its Limits*. Oxford: Oxford University Press.

Williamson, T. (2011). Improbable knowing. In T. Dougherty (ed.), *Evidentialism and Its Discontents*. Oxford: Oxford University Press, pp. 147–64.

Williamson, T. (2019). Evidence of evidence in epistemic logic. In M. Skipper & A. Steglich-Petersen (eds.), Higher-*Order Evidence: New Essays*. Oxford: Oxford University Press, pp. 265–97

Worsnip, A. (2018). The conflict of evidence and coherence. *Philosophy and Phenomenological Research*, *96*(1), 3–44.

Ye, R. (2015). Fumerton's puzzle for theories of rationality. *Australasian Journal of Philosophy*, *93*(1), 93–108.

Ye, R. (2020). Higher-order defeat and intellectual responsibility. *Synthese*, *197*(12), 5435–55.

Cambridge Elements $\equiv$

Epistemology

Stephen Hetherington
University of New South Wales, Sydney

Stephen Hetherington is Professor Emeritus of Philosophy at the University of New South Wales, Sydney. He is the author of numerous books including *Knowledge and the Gettier Problem* (Cambridge University Press, 2016), and *What Is Epistemology?* (Polity, 2019), and is the editor of, most recently, *Knowledge in Contemporary Epistemology* (with Markos Valaris: Bloomsbury, 2019), and *What the Ancients Offer to Contemporary Epistemology* (with Nicholas D. Smith: Routledge, 2020). He was the Editor-in-Chief of the Australasian Journal of Philosophy from 2013 until 2022.

About the Series
This Elements series seeks to cover all aspects of a rapidly evolving field including emerging and evolving topics such as these: fallibilism; knowinghow; self-knowledge; knowledge of morality; knowledge and injustice; formal epistemology; knowledge and religion; scientific knowledge; collective epistemology; applied epistemology; virtue epistemology; wisdom. The series will demonstrate the liveliness and diversity of the field, pointing also to new areas of investigation.

Cambridge Elements ≡

Epistemology

Elements in the Series

Foundationalism
Richard Fumerton

The Epistemic Consequences of Paradox
Bryan Frances

Coherentism
Erik J. Olsson

The A Priori *Without Magic*
Jared Warren

Defining Knowledge
Stephen Hetherington

Wisdom: A Skill Theory
Cheng-hung Tsai

Higher-Order Evidence and Calibrationism
Ru Ye

A full series listing is available at: www.cambridge.org/EEPI